Longford, Frank Pakenham, 7th Earl of, 1905-
    Nixon : a study in extremes of fortune /
Lord Longford. London : Weidenfeld and
Nicolson, c1980.
    ix, 205 p. : ill.
    Bibliography: p. 196-198.

1. Nixon, Richard M. (Richard Milhous),
1913-   2. Presidents - United States -
Biography. 3. United States - Politics and
government - 1945-   I. Title.
0297777084   1143263

39

NIXON

NIXON

A Study in Extremes of Fortune

Lord Longford

Weidenfeld and Nicolson
London

For Elizabeth

First published in Great Britain by
George Weidenfeld and Nicolson Limited
91 Clapham High Street
London SW4 7TA

ISBN 0 297 77708 4

Printed in Great Britain by
Butler & Tanner Ltd
Frome and London

Contents

Illustrations

Foreword

Words without number have been written about President Nixon, but I cannot discover up till now a biography of him which has been published since Watergate. Many people have been kind enough to discuss him with me, some with and some without expert qualifications. I will single out Mr 'Chuck' Colson who read an early draft of this book and made a number of valuable suggestions. Mr Ray Price has also been most kind and helpful. Other opinions, less favourable to the former President, have not been hard to come by.

I have had the pleasure of two long meetings with President Nixon himself, one during the early stages and one when the book was more or less complete. As far as I know he has not seen a copy of the manuscript. I need hardly say that none of those mentioned, or anyone else for that matter, is responsible for any of my interpretations or conclusions.

Yet once more I am deeply grateful to my Personal Assistant, Gwen Keeble, for help in a hundred different ways and to Barbara Winch for her expert typing of the manuscript. My wife, as always, has been involved and indispensable from first to last.

I

From Whittier to the White House

1912–53

It was roses, roses, all the way,
With myrtle mixed in my path like mad:
The house-roofs seemed to heave and sway,
The church-spires flamed, such flags they had,
A year ago on this very day!

A year later:

There's nobody on the house-tops now –
Just a palsied few at the windows set;
For the best of the sight is, all allow,
At the Shambles' Gate – or, better yet,
By the very scaffold's foot, I trow.

In November 1972 Richard Nixon, then aged sixty, had been
before the American public a long time. He had been elected
to the House of Representatives in 1946 and to the Senate
in 1950. He had been Vice-President from 1953 to 1960. In
the latter year he had only failed by a hair's breadth to win
the presidency against John Kennedy. From 1969 to 1972 he
had been President. One would think that the American
public would, by this time, have made up their minds about
him as a political leader and a man.

On 9 November he was re-elected President by a record
margin of votes. Great achievements in the international
sphere lay just behind him; greater ones loomed up in front.

He seemed almost literally on top of the world. One year later, waves of hatred, it has been truly said, from millions of people were crashing down on the White House. Every aspect of his life, political and personal, was being investigated, derided and denigrated. A few months later again he was to be hurled from power amid merciless execration. Yet he was still the same man as was 'The Patriot' in Browning's poem. What kind of man he was, and is, the reader must judge from the narrative that follows.

No human being, least of all one who has become for a time the most powerful man in the world, can be explained entirely in terms of his heredity and environment. Nixon was one of five brothers of whom two died in boyhood and one became bankrupt. There was no reason whatever why Richard should have risen to such incredible heights, achieved so much or met with such disaster, apart from his own special endowment of moral character, mental ability, physical vigour and morally neutral ambition. Yet his background cannot be overlooked, though in fact it is overlooked too often or handled too selectively. His critics, of whom there have always been large supplies, have stressed the fact that he went to Whittier, a small college in California; hence, we are told, his social inferiority complex and his lifelong distrust of the eastern liberal establishment. That analysis may contain an element of truth, but his Quaker background, so often set aside, must be regarded as far more fundamental.

The facts about his birth and upbringing have been summarized more than once by himself. He was born on 9 January 1913 in a small agricultural town called Yorba Linda, thirty miles inland from Los Angeles, California. His mother's family were Quakers; her name was Milhous and she came from a Quaker family that left County Kildare in Ireland in 1729. His father was Irish too. His family was Methodist, but when he married Nixon's mother he became a Quaker.

Richard Nixon says of his parents, no doubt truly, that 'they were both deeply religious'. In later years he would refer to his mother as a 'saint', a description not apparently disputed. She possessed, it seems, a special quality of making people 'want to be close to her'. Though the inner serenity religion gave her shone through, 'she never wore her religion on her sleeve'. His father, a lovable character, must be accounted a worldly failure. The Nixons and Milhouses had lived in America for over two hundred years – farmers, artisans and traders, but in recent times the Nixons had never achieved even moderate wealth.

Richard Nixon was brought up in Whittier, a small Quaker town, his life dominated by family, church and school. The family went to church four times on Sunday and to Wednesday night services as well. During his high school and college years, Nixon played the piano for various church services each week.

Kenneth Harris, interviewing Nixon for the *Observer* in 1968, asked him: 'Were you reasonably well off as children?' and Nixon replied: 'No, the going was hard. When we were kids my mother would be up before dawn making pies to sell in the store.' (He was later to describe his father as a grocer.) 'My father just about made things pay but we boys had to help. We helped prepare meals so that our parents could work in the store, we worked in our spare time for local farmers. When we were old enough we helped with the gasoline pumps.'

Nixon's father, if materially unsuccessful, was a devoted family man. He was also quick-tempered and combative. No one, friend or foe, would deny that throughout his subsequent career Nixon revealed exceptional qualities as a fighter – courage certainly, but combativeness also. The first owed much to both parents, the second to the father alone.

Both parents were equally convinced about the virtues of self-help in various senses. Nixon's family had a deep belief in the 'little' man in America. His favourite Biblical passage was 'in the sweat of thy face shalt thou eat bread'. During the long period when Richard's brother had tuberculosis – the years of the great Depression – his father refused to let him go to the county tuberculosis hospital, one of the best in the country, on the grounds that going there would be taking charity. The father was determined that Richard, the hope of the family, should have the education which he himself had missed. Both parents were delighted with his immense success when it came, but his mother never failed to remind him, even when he had reached a lofty position, that the

3

things of the spirit were nobler than those belonging to this world.

Richard Nixon did well at school. He finished third in his high-school class, won the constitutional oratorical contests in his junior and senior years, and received the Harvard Club of California's award for outstanding all-round student. There was a possibility of a tuition scholarship to Yale, but travel and living expenses would amount to even more than tuition. By 1930 the Depression and the enormous expenses of his brother Harold's illness had stripped the family finances to the bone. He had no choice but to live at home and that meant that he would have to attend Whittier College. 'I was not disappointed because the idea of college was so exciting that nothing could have dimmed it for me.'

At Whittier College Nixon graduated second in his class. He travelled thousands of miles representing Whittier in debates. His happiest memories involved sports, especially football, though he was too light to become a full member of the college team. He was thanked by the coach for his services in one capacity or another. He went on next to the new Duke University Law School in North California, winning in his second year the Presidency of the Duke Bar Association and specializing in constitutional law. In June 1937 he graduated third in his class. He would have liked to find work in New York but nothing came his way. He returned home and obtained a job in Whittier's oldest law firm.

He became involved in amateur dramatics and in those circles met in 1938 a 'beautiful and vivacious young woman with Titian hair', as he calls her in his Memoirs. This was Pat Ryan, one of seven children born in a mining town in Nevada but brought up on a small ranch about twenty miles south-west of Los Angeles – a material background very like Nixon's, though without the special Quaker atmosphere. She was an adventurous girl, taking jobs of various kinds, including secretarial work in New York, but she had always been determined to graduate; she returned to Los Angeles and took her degree with honours at the University of Southern California. When Nixon met her she was teaching business courses at Whittier High School. She was charming students and Faculty alike, so Nixon tells us, and I am sure it was so.

4

Almost at once he asked her for a date. She said, 'I am very busy,' which would have put off a less-determined suitor. He said, 'You shouldn't say that because some day I am going to marry you.' They were in fact married in June 1940, a love match and a loving marriage that never faltered.

Nixon says that his parents were immediately impressed by Pat's obvious strength of character and indomitable spirit. These qualities were to be tested to the utmost in the years ahead by extremes of good and bad fortune, success and failure, both carried to the nth degree. Pat's courage and fidelity were absolute at all times, amid much joy and many sufferings.

By now he was well established in the local community as a rising young lawyer and was approached by several of the town's Republican leaders about running for the State Assembly. But before Pearl Harbor in December 1941 he accepted a job in the Office of Price Administration in Washington. He did not feel that he could sit out the war in Whittier even before the United States were drawn in and, after eight months in Price Administration, he felt impelled to apply for a commission in the Navy. This was sad news for his devoutly pacifist mother, but she respected his decision and no kind of breach occurred.

In August 1942 he was sent to the Naval Officer Indoctrination School at Quonset Point, Rhode Island. After honorable, though not glamorous war service in the South Pacific, he was ordered back to the States in July 1944. ('I wrote Pat every day during the fourteen months I was away.') In September 1945, while still uncertain about his civilian career, he received a letter from one of the Republican leaders of Whittier's community: 'I am writing you this short note to ask if you would like to be a candidate for Congress on the Republican ticket in 1946.' The sitting Congressman, Voorhis, a man of no small distinction and public service, seemed impossible to defeat. Nixon, however, had the great advantage that in 1946 the national trend, or swing as we would call it, was strongly Republican.

After the elections the Republicans had a majority in both houses (though a tiny one in the Senate) for the only time since the beginning of the great Depression, Nixon stressed the socialist aspect of the Voorhis programme and its general left-wing character. The allegation that he spread a whispering campaign that Voorhis was a communist is one he still resents and describes as a 'fairly recent invention of the typewriter pundits'. He insists that communism was not the issue at any time during the 1945 campaign. At the time of resignation the *New York Times*, in a summary of his career, harped on the fact that he had employed a reckless tactic of guilt by association. They gave this example: 'I welcome', said Nixon during the campaign, 'the opposition of PAC [Political Action Committee) with its communist principles and its huge slush funds.' In 1974 the *New York Times* was still pointing out that Voorhis was not endorsed by PAC and that the organization was not a communist one.

Nixon's reply in his memoirs is fairly effective: 'There were in fact two organizations, PAC and NCPAC [National Citizens' Political Action Committee].' According to Nixon, although the leadership of both groups was non-communist the organizations were known to be infiltrated with communists and fellow-travellers. In fact, Voorhis had been endorsed by PAC in 1944 but not in 1946. He was endorsed by NCPAC without his consent. After the matter was raised by Nixon he repudiated the endorsement by either body.

Nixon tried to show his respect to Voorhis after the election. The latter was far from ungenerous to him in his memoirs. Without anticipating much that is to come later, one must say a word here about Nixon's so-called anti-communism; an ambiguous phrase which could cover defence of the West, exposure of communist infiltrators, or positive aggression towards the Soviet Union.

Writing of 1946, Nixon tells us: 'My own attitude towards communism had recently changed from one of general disinterest to one of extreme concern ... it was Churchill's iron curtain speech delivered in Fulton, Missouri, March 1946 that profoundly affected my attitude towards communism in general and the Soviet Union in particular....' In line with this his maiden speech in the House on 18 February 1947 was a presentation of a 'contempt of Congress citation' against Gerhardt Eislet who had been identified as the top communist agent in America. In July 1947 he was 'probably the most

6

surprised man in Washington when he read that he had been chosen by the Speaker to be a member of a select Committee headed by Congressman Herter'. They were to go to Europe and prepare a report in connection with the Foreign Aid plan that the Secretary of State, General Marshall, had just unveiled.

This visit left a permanent mark on Nixon's international thinking. When he was elected President in 1968 he saw that the central factor in American international policy was the same as 'it had been in 1947 when I first went to Europe with the Herter committee'. America now, as then, was the main defender of the free world against the encroachment and aggression of the communist world. He came back from the 1947 visit to Europe with a firm conviction: 'The only thing that the communists would respect and deal with seriously was power at least equal to theirs and backed up by a willingness to use it.' He never wavered from this conviction subsequently, although he came to recognize ever more clearly that this in itself was not a sufficient policy for world peace.

Gerald Ford, his successor as President and friend all through their time together in public life, has some noteworthy things to say about Nixon as a young Congressman. He himself entered the House of Representatives two years after Nixon. 'One of our closest ties', he writes, 'was that we came from middle America (economically if not geographically). . . . We respected each other because each of us knew that the other had come up the hard way . . and all the while our friendship was strengthened by our mutual adherence to the same basic policies at home and abroad. . . . Nixon was an idealistic believer in the American economic and political system.' Nixon, as he came to know him, 'had a brilliant mind, great sensitivities to the public's political mood and the unique ability to analyse foreign policy issues and act decisively on them'.

We come now to the Hiss case which was to have such an enormous influence on Nixon's career and, for good or for ill, his image. Just before the summer recess at the end of July 1943 the House Committee on un-American Activities, of which Nixon was a member, heard testimony from Elizabeth Bentley, an admitted courier for a communist spy ring in

Washington during the war. Following that, Whittaker Chambers, a gifted if eccentric editor of *Time Life* and ex-communist, was called before the Committee in the hope that he might be able to throw light on some of the Bentley revelations. Chambers said that in the 1930s he had been part of a communist group whose primary aim was to infiltrate the government. Among members of this group, he alleged, was Alger Hiss, a well-known and highly respected figure in New York and Washington. After a brilliant record at Harvard Law School, Hiss occupied a number of important government posts in connection with the New Deal. He served as one of President Roosevelt's advisers at the Yalta Conference. He was acknowledged as one of the primary architects of the United Nations, serving as Secretary-General of the San Francisco conference at which the United Nations Charter was drafted. In 1947 he became President of the Carnegie Endowment for International Peace, its Chairman John Foster Dulles recommending his selection.

On 5 August 1948 Hiss came at his own request and testified before the Committee. 'I am not', he said, 'and never have been a member of the Communist Party. I do not, and never have adhered to the tenets of the Communist Party. I am not, and never have been, *a member of any* communist front organization. I have never followed the Communist Party line, directly or indirectly.' He did not even know anyone called Chambers, and as far as he could remember, never had. When he finished his testimony he was besieged by admirers and then and later overwhelmed with public acclamation. Chambers was discredited. So was the Committee. They were now in a bad way, in a panic, in a condition bordering on despair. One of them spoke for the majority when he blurted out, 'We are ruined.' I was', recalled Nixon, 'the only member of the Committee in favour of holding our ground and pursuing the case further.'

They had, after all, little by this time to lose and possibly much to gain by battling on. Nixon had noticed, moreover, that for all the vehemence of his denials, Hiss had not said unequivocally that he had not ever in fact known Chambers. He had used the words 'I had never seen him,' but attached the qualification 'as far as I know'. Nixon again had a feeling

that Hiss was somehow too suave, too smooth, too self-confi-
dent to be an entirely trustworthy witness. Was there any element here of a Whittier prejudice against Harvard? It was
arranged that Nixon and two other members of the Committee should interview Chambers privately. When this was
done the credibility of Chambers was enhanced. Nixon
became convinced that Hiss was lying.

Hiss was called back before the Committee on 16 August.
He became less confident when Nixon concentrated on the
question of whether he had ever known Chambers. He introduced the name of a man he admitted he *had* known,
George Crossley, whom Nixon still calls 'the man that never
was'. Nixon now felt sure that Hiss had indeed known
Chambers, whether or not under the name of Crossley. A confrontation had to be and was duly arranged. It took place in
the first instance in private. There were many moments of
melodrama. Hiss arrived first, then Chambers was brought
in, Nixon taking the lead throughout. Nixon began, 'Mr
Chambers, will you please stand? And will you please stand
Mr Hiss?' The two men stood and Hiss turned to face
Chambers. 'Mr Hiss', went on Nixon, 'the man standing here
is Mr Whittaker Chambers. I ask you now if you have ever
known that man before?'

'I do not think', writes Nixon, 'that I have ever seen one
man look at another with more hatred in his eyes than did
Alger Hiss when he looked at Whittaker Chambers.' Some
tense exchanges followed. At one point Hiss insisted that
Chambers should open his mouth so that he could study the
state of his teeth. Later on he announced: 'I am now perfectly
prepared to identify this man as George Crossley' – whom
he had admittedly known but had *not* known that he was
a communist.

Public confrontation came on 28 August. Hiss stuck to his
story that he had known Chambers as Crossley, though he
carried diminishing conviction under close questioning from
Nixon and others. Later Chambers appeared in a 'Meet the
Press' TV programme. 'Are you willing', he was asked, 'to
repeat your charge that Alger Hiss was a communist?' 'Alger
Hiss was a communist,' he replied, 'and may still be one.' Hiss
was expected to sue Chambers for libel immediately. He did

9

not do so for three weeks to the dismay of his supporters. The ground seemed to be giving away under him.

But there were some surprising twists. Chambers was well aware that in a court of law his case was weak without documentary proof. On 17 November he produced an envelope containing sixty-five pages of typewritten copies of State Department documents and four memos in Alger Hiss's handwriting. When Chambers decided to leave the Communist Party he had hidden these papers away as a protection against any communist attempts to blackmail or kill him. But the outcome of his producing these documents was the opposite of what he and Nixon had expected. The word went round that it was not Hiss but Chambers who was to be prosecuted for perjury, on the grounds that he had lied when he testified that he himself had never been involved in espionage. And it was now clear from his own documents that he had been. Nixon at this precise moment was badly placed to help him. His second daughter Julie had been born in July. He had promised Pat a fortnight's Caribbean holiday as soon as Congress went into recess. Before he set off Chambers told him that he was keeping a real bombshell up his sleeve. After a more or less sleepless night, Nixon arranged for a subpoena to be served on Chambers for the rest of his material.

Nixon's holiday was almost at once interrupted. Messages reached him that the new Chambers material was 'incredibly hot'. He came dashing back to encounter the greatest sensation yet. Chambers had explained to the investigators that he had not wanted to leave anything in his house in case subpoenas or search warrants arrived in his absence. He had therefore hollowed out a pumpkin and placed in it a large collection of microfilms. When the pumpkin microfilms were developed, they yielded hundred of tapes of photostats, a selection of the classified documents Hiss gave to Chambers, in the period just before Chambers left the party. This time Hiss was really undone. The Statute of Limitations made prosecuting for espionage impossible but the Grand Jury unanimously decided to indict Hiss on two counts of perjury. Eventually Hiss was found guilty and sentenced to five years' imprisonment.

President Truman had tried to ridicule the pursuit of Hiss as a red herring. When all was over he commented privately:

'Of course Hiss is guilty. But that damn committee is not interested in Hiss. All it cares about is politics and as long as they try to make politics out of the communist issue I am going to label their activities for what they are, a red herring.' Hiss, however, has never failed to protest his innocence and must, to say the least, be given the highest marks for persistence. A book comes out every few years on the case, one a year since Watergate brought discredit on his leading antagonist.

The most comprehensive and thoroughgoing work yet published, *Perjury* by Professor Allen Weinstein, appeared in 1978. The author began by believing that Hiss was innocent but finished by concluding unequivocally that Hiss was guilty as charged. He is far from kind to Nixon, against whom he reveals a good deal of personal animosity. He describes him as an 'active negative type', a personality that ordinarily displays twin sets of impulses – 'the struggle to control aggression, and the pursuit of power, prestige and status'. Without serious evidence he asserts that Nixon nursed a suppressed and intensely felt personal antagonism towards Alger Hiss. He labours Nixon's alleged obsession with his triumph over Hiss right up to the end of his presidency. None of that matters very much.

But what follows is more serious and will demand a reply from Nixon in due course. According to Weinstein, Nixon had excellent reason *before* the Hiss case came up to believe in Hiss's communist affiliations. He had had several meetings earlier with a Catholic priest named John Cronin who specialized in collecting data on communist infiltration. All this if true would prove nothing in Hiss's favour but it would diminish the credit due to Nixon for his courage and foresight in going forward when the odds seemed so heavily against him. It would also imply a certain lack of candour on his part.

Be all that as it may, there can be no doubt that, as a direct result of the Hiss case, Nixon became a national figure while still only thirty-six. The fact that he was Vice-President within four years suggests that in any case his political capacity and drive towards the top would have brought him forward sooner rather than later, but without the Hiss case he would hardly have been elected a Senator so early as 1950.

It will be seen from the sequence of events described above that it did not need the Hiss case to make him a militant anti-communist. He was that already. It would be quite unfair to imply that he took up the Hiss case primarily for personal reasons. The case brought him rapid advancement and permanent support in conservative quarters. But he paid a heavy price from then onwards to the end. Bill Safire writes, 'Since Nixon appeared on the national scene riding the tide of anti-communism he has been criticized and maligned by Washington commentators, who generally were liberal in their political leanings. His success in the Hiss case, proving he was right and the liberals who refused to believe him were wrong, only reinforced the bitter resentments against him.' If Nixon became something of a hero hereafter to anti-communists, he was type-cast from now on in the eyes of the eastern liberal establishment as an illiberal and ruthless reactionary. Henceforth they pursued him with undying hostility to which he reacted with equal ferocity. The escalating mutual antagonism was to play a large part in his life story. His long-standing opponents 'put the boot in' or, in his own phrase, 'stuck in the sword' he gave them when their chance came and greeted his fall with unalloyed satisfaction.

Richard Nixon was not one to let the grass grow under his feet. He soon began to consider the possibility of moving upwards. David Halberstam (*The Powers That Be*) lays great stress on the support given to Nixon in those early years by the *Los Angeles Times*. (Their attitude was to become much more equivocal later.) They had powerfully attacked Voorhis during the campaign of 1946. Now, in late 1949, the key man, Kyle Palmer, called Nixon in Washington and asked: 'Dick, have you thought of running for the Senate?' In Halberstam's words: 'The oligarchy was all lined up, a few more phone calls were made, the money was arranged.' Halberstam cannot be treated as infallible, least of all in regard to Nixon, for whom he has never a good word. But what he says is significant here. Nearly all Nixon's political friends told him that running for the Senate would be tantamount to political suicide, but in his usual shrewd way he recognized the worth of the nation-wide publicity that the Hiss case had given him. Without his seeking it, but certainly without his avoiding it, he had achieved within two years of entering the House of Representatives publicity on a scale that most Congressmen only dreamt of achieving, if at all, after years of service. California's Democratic Senator would be finishing his term in 1950. The prospects of beating him were not at first sight promising. Downey was a popular and uncontroversial incumbent; nevertheless Nixon determined to challenge him.

A new and, from his point of view, favourable element came into the situation when Representative Helen Gahagan Douglas announced that she was going to run against Downey in the Democratic primary. This was excellent news for Nixon. If Downey won the primary he would be weakened by her attacks. If Mrs Douglas won she would be easier to beat than Downey. Helen Douglas, however, was no mean opponent. She had been a popular light opera and Broadway musical star during the 1920s. She was as hard-hitting in her way as Nixon in his. Senator Downey soon withdrew on health grounds and the ring was ready for two strong competitors.

Jack Kennedy, five years younger but his contemporary in the House, called on Nixon. 'Dick', he said, 'I know you are in for a pretty rough campaign and my father wanted to help you out.' He left behind $1,000 – handsome to say the least from a political opponent. The gift and its reception seem to reflect mutual credit on the millionaire's son and the young man without resources, though I have never come across such an episode in English politics and, if known, it would be highly suspect.

Jack Kennedy had been right in forecasting a rough campaign. The *New York Times* reported: 'Mrs Douglas has been depicting her opponent as a red-baiting, reactionary enemy of labour and the common man. . . . Mr Nixon has been assailing Mrs Douglas as a flighty left-winger and an exponent of a regime that failed.' Nixon won the election by a majority of 680,000 votes, the largest plurality of any Senate winner that year. Senator Downey, the retiring Democratic Senator, sent him a telegram: 'Please accept my congratulations on your notable victory and my best wishes and regards.' Jack Kennedy told an informal gathering of professors and students at Harvard that he was personally very happy that Nixon had defeated Mrs Douglas.

But as in most of his campaigns Nixon was accused of hitting too hard. He had certainly announced, 'We must put on a fighting, rocking, socking campaign.' He still insists that he stuck to *issues* and that so far as he attacked Mrs Douglas he did so on her record and her views. The truth is that Nixon was a fighter first, last and always, a quality which, throughout, brought him immense support and intense hostility. At a lunch over which I was presiding in London in 1978 he told half-seriously what he called a humorous story which certainly produced plenty of laughter. He had been announcing a policy of 'doing to others what they do to us' when Henry Kissinger chipped in: 'Plus 10 per cent.' Nixon always, I am sure, assumed that in the mighty contests of top-level politics one went all-out to win within certain recognized conventions. He assumed, I would think correctly, that his conventions were not different from those of Roosevelt, Truman, Kennedy or Johnson, to go no further back. But he certainly left plenty of scars.

Nixon's chariot rolled forward. There seemed to be no stopping him. He was elected Senator at the end of 1950. By the middle of 1952 he was being seriously considered as a Vice-Presidential candidate. On 1 July he flew to Chicago for the Republican National Convention. It began to be predicted that Eisenhower and Nixon would be the Republican nominees, and so it proved. Eisenhower wanted his campaign to be waged as a crusade against the corruption of the Truman administration which he asserted had played into the communists' hands both in Europe and in Asia. Clearly he envisaged taking an above-the-battle position. What was needed for the hard partisan campaigning was an upstanding young man who was a good aggressive speaker. Nixon should be able not only to pillory the Democrats on the corruption issue but also to personify the remedy for it. As for the communist threat, Eisenhower said that the Hiss case was a text from which Nixon could preach unlimited sermons. To maintain his sublime position, Eisenhower needed a running mate who revelled in all-out combat and excelled at it. In Nixon's expressive phrase, 'the hero needed a point man'.

Nixon was duly selected as Vice-Presidential candidate.

Among thousands of congratulatory letters there was one from Jack Kennedy:

Dear Dick:
I was tremendously pleased that the convention selected you for V.P. I was always convinced that you would move ahead to the top – but I never thought it would come this quickly. You were an ideal selection and will bring to the ticket a great deal of strength.
Please give my best to your wife and all kinds of good luck to you.
Cordially,
Jack Kennedy

Then suddenly, out of a blue sky, a storm blew up which threatened to destroy Nixon's whole political career. Nixon calls it in his memoirs the Fund Crisis and devotes to it no less than eighteen pages; roughly the same as he gives to the Hiss case. In 1961 he was to produce his massive book *Six Crises* in which both these two were included. But there is no doubt that up to the time of Watergate the Fund Crisis caused him, and particularly Pat, more pain than all the other crises put together. Quite unexpectedly, after a broadcast, a columnist took him aside and said, 'What is this fund we hear about? There is a rumour to the effect that you have a supplementary salary of 22,000 dollars contributed by a hundred California businessmen.' Later Pat summed up the unfairness of the whole thing: 'Not only isn't the fund illegal but you know how you bent over backwards to make sure that every cent was accounted for.' In the event it was proved beyond argument by independent inquiry that Nixon had not personally profited from the fund.

For a long time, however, his political opponents managed to give quite a different impression to the nation. Within a few days the whole nation was humming with stories and rumours about the Nixon Fund and with speculations about Nixon's future. The *Washington Post*, already his confirmed enemy, called for his resignation. What was much more serious was that the *Herald Tribune* did the same; it was generally considered to be the most influential Republican paper in the east, if not in the country. Nixon knew that the publisher and editor were close to Eisenhower. Things looked grim for Nixon.

Pat was inflexible against his resigning. Unless Richard fought for his honour in the face of such an attack, he would mar not only his own life but the lives of his family, particularly Tricia and Julie. Eisenhower, when questioned, adopted an equivocal posture. He refused to condemn Nixon but added, 'Of what avail is it for us to carry on this crusade against this business of what has been going on in Washington, if we ourselves are not as clean as a hound's tooth?' The implication circulated widely that Eisenhower was not yet certain that Nixon was as clean as a hound's tooth. The latter's mother in Washington, looking after the girls, sent two telegrams. One, to Nixon, read: 'Girls are okay.' The other telegram, which Nixon did not hear about for a few days, went to Eisenhower: 'Dear General: I am trusting that the absolute truth may come out concerning this attack on Richard, and when it does I am sure you will be guided right in your decision, to place implicit faith in his integrity and honesty. Best wishes from one who has known Richard longer than anyone else. His mother.'

Perhaps no other mother would have written that telegram, but there cannot have been many mothers like her. The next day, Sunday, there was still no direct word from Eisenhower, and Nixon learnt that the circle round Eisenhower was by now a 'hanging jury'. Eventually, when Eisenhower telephoned, his attitude was cryptic. 'I have come to the conclusion', he said, 'that you are the one who has to decide what to do. After all, you've got a big following in this country, and if the impression got around that you got off the ticket because I forced you off, it is going to be very bad. On the other hand, if I issue a statement now backing you up, in effect people will accuse me of condoning a wrongdoing.' Hardly Eisenhower's finest message.

He followed up with one equally infuriating, though it made fairly good sense: 'I don't want to be in the position of condemning an innocent man. Tell them everything there is to tell, everything you can remember since the day you entered public life. Tell them about any money you have ever received.' Pressed by Nixon, he still would not promise an announcement one way or another. On the telephone Nixon used language to Eisenhower that caused some surprise.

'There comes a time', he said, 'in matters like this when you have either got to shit or come off the pot.' But Eisenhower was still not ready to commit himself. His last words were, 'Keep your chin up.'

Then came the television programme when Nixon delivered the most effective address of his life. He set out the facts about the fund and his personal finances. He engaged in a counter-attack against Stevenson, whose own finances seemed at least as much open to question. He praised Eisenhower and then requested that his audience send letters and wires to the Republican National Committee in Washington to say whether they thought he should remain on the ticket or step down. His speech was bitterly criticized afterwards by his opponents because of what they considered the crude exploitation of sentiment. 'Pat doesn't have a mink coat,' he said, working in a reference to Democratic scandals, 'but she does have a respectable Republican cloth coat.' He referred ironically to Checkers, a dog his children had received as a gift. This reference to Checkers drove his opponents to the point of apoplexy. But everybody must choose their own brand of sentiment. Nixon's love of his family was a totally genuine emotion. He was fully entitled to present himself at his crisis of his fortunes as a dedicated family man and appeal to millions of other Americans at the point of their deepest loyalties. His success was overwhelming.

Eisenhower's telegram of congratulations did not reach him initially. When Eisenhower invited him to meet him at Wheeling, West Virginia, Nixon was doubtful whether he would humiliate himself further. He was told that the General had said that one speech was not enough. But on reflection, he persuaded himself that Eisenhower's request was reasonable. When they landed at Wheeling a joyful surprise awaited them. 'The General is coming up the steps', said Nixon's friend, Murray Chotiner, with awe in his voice. Eisenhower strode down the aisle, hand outstretched, flashing his famous smile. 'General', said Nixon, 'you did not need to come out to the airport.' 'Why not?' he replied grinning. 'You're my boy.' And so it all ended happily in terms of Nixon's career. Eisenhower, with Nixon beside him, went forward to a great election victory by 55.1 to 44.4 per cent.

Nixon's mother quietly took him aside and gave him a small piece of paper on which she had written a message: 'To Richard: You have gone far and we are proud of you always – I know that you will keep your relationship with your Maker as it should be, for after all, that, as you must know, is the most important thing in this life.'

But Nixon had not enjoyed the election. He was not surprised that the story about the fund was exploited by his political opponents, but he was disappointed and hurt that so many Republicans pre-judged him without waiting for the facts and he was bitterly disillusioned by the performance of the press. 'I regarded what had been done to me as character assassination, and the experience permanently and powerfully affected my attitude toward the press in particular and the news media in general.' He tells us also that he learnt what he calls 'some important lessons' about politics and friendship: 'In politics most people are your friends, only as long as you can do something for them or something to them.' He tries to be philosophical. Perhaps other walks of life in this respect are much the same as politics, 'but the openly competitive nature of politics probably makes that fact stand out more starkly.'

What was the moral to be learnt from the behaviour towards him of Eisenhower, perhaps the most respected American of the century? The duty of the real statesman, it might seem, was to put public consideration before all feelings of personal friendship and loyalty. Nixon henceforth became more sophisticated; better equipped for jungle warfare. Already a hard fighter, he may have been hardened excessively by this searing experience.

Theodore White, author of the invaluable series of books entitled *The Making of the President*, finds a further significance in Nixon's 1952 experience. 'One must mark 1952 as the date that Richard Nixon discovered how spectacular the influence of television could be, when, with his masterful and era-marking 'Checkers speech', he reached for the first time, nationally, to stir the emotions of Middle America and override the decision of the party masters for his dismissal.... Television would change the mechanics of all future campaigning, inviting in the manipulators.' But it can be argued just as easily that it was the Kennedy men who introduced the whole new style of public relations into American presidential politics. It was Joe Kennedy, not Nixon's father, who said of his son 'we will package him like soap'.

2

The Penultimate Pedestal
1953–60

Nixon was a Vice-President for eight years, from the beginning of 1953 till the end of 1960. Vice-Presidents seldom make their mark on history unless they suddenly turn into Presidents, but Nixon's vice-presidency was full of the colour of his 'Six Crises'.

Of these we have already encountered two, the Fund agony and the Hiss Case. The remaining four we will come to later: the Eisenhower heart-attack (1955), the horrid experience at Caracas (1958), the conflict with Khrushchev (1959) and the defeat by Kennedy (1960). Throughout the period there was his steady development as an international statesman, actual and potential.

There was one thread running through Nixon's vice-presidency which must be disentangled, the rather ambivalent attitude to him of Eisenhower and the rather peculiar relationship resulting. Nixon had good reason to be grateful to Eisenhower. It was Eisenhower who, by his personal fiat, had lifted this young man of forty to the vice-presidency of the United States. Eisenhower, as we have already seen, wanted someone other than himself to do the hard aggressive electioneering and generally say and do the unpopular things while his own image remained intact above the battle.

Nixon reports a conversation with General Walter Bedell Smith, Eisenhower's Chief of Staff in the Second World War. Smith uncharacteristically blurted out his pent-up feelings on one occasion when he was very tired: 'I was just Ike's prat boy,' he said. 'Ike always had to have a prat boy, someone who'd do the dirty work for him. He always had to have someone else who could do the firing or the reprimanding, or give any orders which he knew people would find unpleasant to carry out. Ike always has to be the nice guy. That's the way it is in the White House, and the way it will always be in any kind of an organization that Ike runs.'

As we shall see, Nixon wearied at times of bearing the brunt of the political antagonisms which had to be deflected from Eisenhower. But in fairness to Eisenhower, there is no doubt that one reason why Nixon was selected for his exhalted role was that he evidently enjoyed giving hard knocks and more than most people was ready to put up with the reactions.

He tells a revealing story. It refers to the 1956 election but it applies generally during these years. He is proud rather than ashamed of it, if we can judge by his memoirs. In 1948 Harry Truman had campaigned to cries of 'Give 'em Hell!' Eisenhower's parting admonition to Nixon in 1956 was: 'Give 'em Heaven.' He followed this advice to begin with, but it proved a complete flop. The press corps and the Republicans were equally disappointed. After a 'Give 'em Heaven' speech, which left the audience deflated, he retired to bed but could not sleep all night. At 5.30 am he got up and set to work on some hard-hitting additions to his basic speech: 'Suddenly I felt as if a great weight had been lifted off me. I had not realized how frustrating it had been to suppress the normal partisan instincts.' His new speech delighted audiences everywhere. He refers to 'the normal partisan instincts' – one could re-write that to read 'my normal partisan instincts'. He cannot, even now, avoid defending himself on the grounds of the malicious ridicule and wild charges of Stevenson. But there is no doubt that in those years he was *par excellence* a no holds barred competitor.

Eisenhower was generous and far-sighted in giving Nixon exceptional opportunities in international affairs. In 1978 I took the chair for him at the Hyde Park Hotel, London, when he addressed a large and sophisticated lunch-time audience. He joined me in receiving perhaps a hundred guests, almost all complete strangers. I was struck by the immediacy of his response to each individual. Over lunch we had quite a good talk. Afterwards he answered questions on international politics for a long while. The audience, whether pro- or anti-Nixon or previously neutral, was agreed that his sheer knowledge and grasp of the world scene were deeply impressive and might not be equalled by anyone now living. He would certainly make a magnificent professor of international politics in any university in any country. His immense knowledge of the subject and his unflagging interest in it, whatever the state of his own fortunes, derived initially from the opportunities given him by Eisenhower.

In the spring of 1953 Eisenhower asked him to undertake a major trip to Asia and the Far East. Accompanied by Pat, he visited no less than thirteen countries: Australia, New Zealand, Indonesia, Malaya, Cambodia, Laos and Vietnam (the last three still forming French Indo-China), Formosa, South Korea, the Philippines, Burma, India and Pakistan. The details need not detain us now, though his personal comments make good reading even today. The journey primarily concerns us in its effect on Nixon's thinking then and later. He himself says that the 1953 trip 'had a tremendously important effect on my thinking and on my career'. He refers to it as an undisputed success at the time and continues, 'It established my Foreign Policy experience and expertise in what was to become the most critical and controversial part of the world.'

Undoubtedly Nixon learnt much about Asia, but what general conclusions could he be said to have drawn? He saw three centuries of colonialism on its death bed. He felt that he was able to diagnose the illness: 'I saw how the leaders and the masses of Asia longed for independence – whether or not they were ready for it, and whether or not they really understood it – because for them it meant dignity and respect. It meant being taken seriously and treated decently, and that was what they wanted.' Today he admits that it is a platitude to say that the peoples of Asia wanted to be treated with respect, but it was a lesson at that time which he thought the European nations had learnt very imperfectly; the British in Malaya under General Templar impressed him much more favourably than the French in Indo-China.

The other main lesson would today be regarded as more controversial and not so obviously beneficial. It became clear to him that if the United States did not 'move' the Chinese, or the Soviets, acting through local communist insurgent groups, certainly would. At that time China and Russia were still good friends. The task of resisting them would ultimately fall to the United States. There was no one else to perform it.

Now comes the unedifying tale of Senator Joe McCarthy. From February 1950 to December 1954 his baleful influence was felt throughout American politics. In February 1950, three years before Nixon became Vice-President, McCarthy gave a stirring address on communist infiltration of government. He brandished a paper which he said contained a list of individuals employed by the State Department who were known to the Secretary of State as members of the Communist Party. And so he proceeded, stepping up his charges with no little support among the American public. In January 1954, four years after his original outburst, 50 per cent of the public had a favourable opinion of McCarthy and only 29 per cent had an unfavourable one.

Nixon, in his own way the leading anti-communist, was considerably embarrassed by the extravagance of McCarthy's hyper-activity in the same area. Looking back, he says of McCarthy: 'He was sincere, and I know from personal investigation that there was real substance to some of his charges. But he could not resist grossly exaggerating his facts.' Making allowance for an element of compassion here towards a once-mighty man now totally discredited. One would be happier if Nixon had managed a stronger condemnation. The fact that the most vehement opponents of McCarthy were over the years hostile and unfair to him no doubt explains a good deal.

Before Eisenhower was elected, McCarthy had been talking about twenty years of treason; in 1954 he began referring to twenty-one years of treason, thus including the first year of Eisenhower's administration. The pace he set himself was too hot to last. When he began attacking the Army with his usual venom he brought Eisenhower down against him – in the end decisively. Not for the only time, Eisenhower saw an astute way to make use of Nixon. 'Dick', he remarked, 'can sometimes take positions which are more political than it would be expected that I take. The difficulty with the McCarthy problem is that anybody who takes it on runs the risk of being called a Pink. Dick has had experience in the communist field and therefore he would not be subject to criticism.' He asked Nixon to undertake a major speech against the Senator.

Nixon fully understood the tactics that Eisenhower was following, but saw no way to escape an unwelcome duty. His speech was, in the event, hailed by Eisenhower as a great success. An extract can be reproduced here as a specimen of the rougher kind of speech Nixon was wont to deliver at the time: 'I have heard people say,' he declared. 'After all we are dealing with a bunch of rats,' [meaning the communists]. 'What we ought to do is to go out and shoot them', [meaning that McCarthy was on the right lines]. Well I agree they are a bunch of rats. But just remember this. When you go out to shoot rats, you have to shoot straight, because when you shoot wildly, it not only means that rats may get away more easily – but you might hit someone else who is trying to shoot rats, too. So, we have to be fair – for two very good reasons: one, because it is right; and two, because it is the most effective way of doing the job.'

McCarthy's embroilment with the Army became more and more savage. Nixon tried to act as a mediator at one point, but ineffectively. Finally from 22 April to 17 June the bitter row between the Army and McCarthy was fought out before the gaze of the public in the Senate Caucas Room. There could only be one winner. On 30 July Senator Flanders introduced a resolution censuring McCarthy. Nixon as Vice-President was presiding over the Senate when the final debate began on 2 December. The final vote was 67 to 62. Joe McCarthy became the third Senator here to be censured by his colleagues.

This same year, 1954, was a significant one for the world and for Nixon. It was the year when the question arose in Vietnam as to whether France would be long able to continue the fight against Ho Chi Minh's communist guerrillas. American policy at that time was based on the vital importance of maintaining an independent Vietnam. The principle was already being accepted of what Eisenhower later called the 'Falling Domino'. The loss of any single country would probably lead to relatively swift submission of an alignment with communism of the remaining countries of the group.

The American public were far from convinced of the importance of preserving the French outpost of Dien Bien Phu and Dulles tried in vain to secure British and French support for concerted opposition to the communists. On 7 May Dien Bien Phu was overrun. It became clear that the French would probably soon be forced to withdraw from Vietnam and America would either have to take over the burden of stopping communist aggression in Indo-China or abandon the whole region. On 21 July a peace settlement was reached in Indo-China, but Foster Dulles, the Secretary of State, was disgusted with the surrender of half Vietnam to the communists. The United States therefore refused to sign the settlement. Nixon agreed with this course, having indeed urged it on Dulles.

The 1954 mid-term elections were rather a painful affair for Nixon. Eisenhower had no taste for the campaign. Nixon had little for it himself: 'The agony of the Fund Crisis had stripped the fun and excitement of campaigning for me.' The wounds suffered two years earlier had gone very deep. Eisenhower wrote him an effusive letter at the end: 'Whenever my burden tends to feel unduly heavy I admire all the more the tremendous job you have done since the opening of the campaign. . . . Please tell Pat that she has aroused my admiration as an able campaigner; there is no question but that she is the most charming of the lot.'

Nixon, who had worked his heart out, was somewhat consoled. The election's results were not unexpected: the Republicans lost sixteen seats in the House and two in the Senate and the Democrats regained control of the House and Senate. Eisenhower, despite his enormous personal popularity, had to deal with a Democrat Congress for the last six years of his presidency. And the long-term prospect was not inviting for Nixon. Clearly Eisenhower was going to maintain this 'President-of-all-the-people' posture. It was Nixon who would be out in front, 'a target of opportunity'. The more effective he became as a campaigner, the more he would attract the slings and arrows. 'The girls were reaching an impressionable age and neither Pat nor I wanted their father to become the perennial bad guy of American politics.' As he flew back to Washington on election day he told his intimate ally Murray Chotiner: 'After this I am through with politics.' He was still only forty-two.

But things did not turn out that way. On 24 September he received a totally unexpected telephone call from the President's Press Secretary: 'This is Jim Hagerty. I have had some bad news. The President has had a coronary.' Hagerty rang off with the words, 'Dick, let me know where you can be reached at all times.' Nixon was staggered, alike by concern for Eisenhower and by the problem of how he himself was to behave in an unprecedented national crisis. As he lay awake that night (there are a large number of references to sleepless nights in his memoirs) he went over and over his future course.

If Eisenhower were soon going to be back on the job it would be foolish for him to do anything that the press could interpret in any way as self-seeking. If Eisenhower died or could not carry on, it would be even more important that Nixon, his automatic successor, should have behaved beforehand with absolute rectitude. In any half-way situation with Eisenhower unable to perform his full duties for a considerable period of time, Nixon must on no account give the impression that he was seeking his power.

A group, including Nixon, of those closest to the President did not believe at that point that Eisenhower would run again. A Gallup poll taken at about this time indicated that if Eisenhower did *not* run Nixon was first choice for the presidential nomination. But forty-eight hours after his heart attack, Eisenhower flew back to Washington. The country, in Nixon's words, seemed to breathe a sigh of relief. There was no more need to worry, Ike was back. Eisenhower's heart attack caused Nixon to modify his attitude to leaving politics. Whether Eisenhower ran or did not run, Nixon was obviously much closer to the presidency. In the event Nixon did run again, as vice-presidential candidate in 1956. But on this occasion he owed nothing to Eisenhower's support. At the end of 1955 Eisenhower actually suggested to him that in his own interests he might be better not to run for Vice-President this time, but to seek instead a Cabinet position. Nixon had a shrewd idea that Eisenhower's intimates were trying to push him off the ticket.

Profiting from his 1952 experience, he said at a subsequent meeting, 'If you believe in your own candidacy and your administration would be better served with me off the ticket, you tell me what you want me to do and I'll do it. I want to do what is best for you.' And so it went on, with Nixon becoming more and more disillusioned. He came close to drafting his resignation but was persuaded not to do so as it would split the Republican Party. Various intrigues threatened his position on the ticket, but in the end he was formally endorsed for nomination.

Just about this time he learnt that his father had suffered a ruptured abdominal artery and was not expected to live. He dashed to his bedside in Whittier. His father was concerned about some manoeuvres by an eminent figure called Harold Stassen which threatened Richard. He knew where Nixon ought to be at such a moment: 'You get back there Dick, to San Francisco and don't let that Stassen pull any last-minute funny business on you.' His father died soon afterwards. But by that time he knew that Dick had been re-nominated by a vote of 1,323 to 1. Eisenhower, with Nixon beside him, had one of the biggest landslides in the presidential history, but he was the first President in 108 years who could not carry the House of Congress for his party – a sombre thought for Nixon with his eyes set on 1960. During the election three foreign crises erupted: on 19 October a brief revolt broke out in communist Poland; on 23 October the Hungarian Revolution began in Budapest; on 5 November, the day before the American election, British and French paratroops landed in Egypt – the Suez Crisis had begun.

In regard to the last of these, Nixon's comments published in 1978 are noteworthy. Eisenhower and Dulles put heavy pressure on Britain, France and Israel to withdraw their forces from Suez: 'In retrospect I believe that our actions were a serious mistake.' In his view, Britain and France were so humiliated and discouraged by the Suez Crisis that they lost their will to play a major role on the world scene. From this time forward, the United States would be forced 'to go it alone' in the foreign policy leadership of the free world. Nixon's reflections on international affairs are usually, whether or not one agrees with them, deeply pondered; I cannot pay that tribute to the comments recorded above. Can he seriously believe today that a trilogy of Britain, France and the USA could have made peace more secure in the Middle East if they had sought to maintain the old colonialist relationships? There were a good many happenings that we can do no more than touch on. There was Operation Mercy 1956, when Nixon flew out to Austria to help the refugees from the Hungarian revolt after its suppression by the Russians. There were President Eisenhower's stroke on 28 November 1957 and the resignation of Sherman Adams, the top man on Eisenhower's staff, in August 1958, an affair in which Nixon was once again called on to play an unattractive role.

But he was given a much more glamorous if all too exciting role when he visited South America in the spring of 1958. Cordial receptions were given in Uruguay, Argentina, Paraguay and Bolivia. But in Peru things became very unpleasant. The communists had openly boasted that they would stop him from getting there. The Rector of the University and the Chief of Police had let it be known that they hoped that he would cancel the visit. But after another of his sleepless nights he decided to go through with it as arranged. 'For two blocks before we reached the gates of San Marcos, we could hear the thousands of demonstrators chanting, '*Fuera* Nixon! *Fuera* Nixon!' – 'Go Home Nixon!' Sometimes the chant became '*Muera* Nixon! *Muera* Nixon!' – 'Death to Nixon!' He walked towards the wall of screaming demonstrators shouting, 'I want to talk to you, why are you afraid of the truth?' A shower of rocks descended on him and his party. At the Catholic University itself they received a tremendous ovation. But when they returned to the hotel the demonstrators were waiting for them. One of them spat in Nixon's face. Pat rushed over and embraced him saying, 'It wasn't just hate that those people had in their eyes. It was a sort of frenzy that frightened me.'

The worst was still awaiting them, however. In Venezuela, when they landed at Maiquetia Airport, the reception was highly hostile. As they entered Caracas they were again pelted with rocks. A mob ran out from the side streets and alleys, and the way forward was completely blocked. The Venezuelan motor-cycle escort evaporated. Twelve secret-service agents struggled desperately to fend off the mob. The first rock hit the car window, spraying them with tiny slivers. A thug with an iron pipe tried to break the window. Once again the glass held, but flying slivers hit them all, including Nixon. The crowd began rocking the car back and forth, slower and higher each time. Each of them realized that they might actually be killed. At last the press truck in front managed to clear a path for them and they shot away to safety. Mercifully Pat's car, just behind Nixon's, had been ignored by the demonstrators. He had been trapped for only twelve minutes, writes Nixon, 'but it seemed like a life-time'. The rest of the trip, while dangerous by ordinary standards, was something of an anti-climax.

On his return to Washington, Nixon found himself more unreservedly popular than at any time previously. Neither he nor Pat could appear anywhere in public without people standing up to applaud. For the first time he pulled even with Kennedy in the Presidential Gallup Trial Heat Polls. In other respects 1958 was a bad year. Eisenhower as usual adopted his posture of lofty detachment. The defeat of the Republicans was shattering. Four November 1958 was one of the most depressing election nights Nixon had ever known. The Democrats increased their majority by 47 seats, thus outnumbering the Republicans by 282 to 153. In the Senate they increased their majority by 13 seats, bringing up the proportion to 62 to 35. We must not forget these figures in assessing Nixon's performance in so nearly winning the presidential election in 1960.

In July 1959 Nixon set off for Moscow to represent the United States at the opening of the American National Exhibition. Only a few highlights can be given here. Khrushchev launched into a tirade against a recent resolution of Congress. Nixon tried to deflect him by quoting President Eisenhower: 'We have beaten this horse to death, let's change to another. Perhaps that's what you and I should do now.' But Khrushchev was not to be disposed of so easily. 'This resolution', he asseverated, 'stinks; it stinks like fresh horse shit and nothing stinks worse than that.'

Nixon was not to be outdone in rudery. He remembered that Khrushchev, in his youth, had worked as a herder of pigs. He also remembered that horse manure was commonly used as fertilizer, but that a neighbour had once used a load of pig manure and the stench was overpowering. He looked Khrushchev straight in the eye and retorted, 'I am afraid the chairman is mistaken. There is something that smells worse than horse shit – and that is pig shit.' For a moment Khrushchev hovered on the borderline of rage. Then he suddenly burst into a broad smile: 'Perhaps you are right there. Perhaps we should talk about something else.'

There were two sharp encounters to come. The first, at the American Exhibition, was in a model television studio. Khrushchev boasted, 'We have existed not quite forty-two years and in another seven years we will be on the same level as America. When we catch up with you, in passing you by we will wave to you . . .' Nixon insisted that Khrushchev must not be 'afraid of ideas. . . . After all, you don't know everything.' Khrushchev shouted furiously, 'If I don't know everything, you don't know anything about communism except fear of it!'

The most controversial attraction was a full-size model of a middle-class American home. Khrushchev refused to believe Nixon when he told him that this might be owned by an American steel worker. An exchange followed which turned into a debate that Nixon says, fairly enough, reverberated round the world. A dramatic photograph was widely circulated in America, to Nixon's great advantage, in which he was prodding Khrushchev's chest with his finger for emphasis Khrushchev accused Nixon of issuing an ultimatum: 'You want to threaten; we will answer threats with threats.' Later he calmed down: 'We want peace and friendship with all nations, especially America.' To this Nixon replied, 'We want peace too.' A young party official was standing beside Khrushchev called Leonid Brezhnev, with whom ten years later Nixon was to strike up a very different relationship.

There were other exchanges, one of them lasting five hours. In all of them Khrushchev boasted loud and long about

Soviet strength, though he was well aware at that time that his country was much weaker than America. Nixon kept his cool and gave nothing away. He made an attempt to discover whether Khrushchev would be prepared to meet President Eisenhower but he got no response. In an unprecedented radio and television address to the Soviet Union, he was adamant in stating his preference for the American system, but he added some conciliatory words: 'We prefer our system. But the very essence of our belief is that we do not and will not try and impose our system on anybody else. We believe that you and all other peoples on this earth should have the right to choose the kind of economic or political system which best fits your particular problems without any foreign intervention.' When Nixon got back home he found that his Russian visit had given him an enormous boost. He had appeared before the eyes of all as the man who had stood up to Khrushchev and, moreover, as one who replied to coarse bluster with dignity and self-control – every American's idea of how their champion should behave in the enemy camp.

Soon it was election year. There was no doubt by now that Nixon would be the Republican candidate. He had always assumed, correctly, that Kennedy would be the Democratic nominee. The stage was set for a campaign of exceptional intensity. Nixon records that 'Jack Kennedy and I were both in the peak years of our political energies; we were contesting great issues in a watershed period of American life and history'. Certainly the personal contrast between the boy from a poor Quaker home in the far west and the Catholic son of a multi-millionaire, with a Harvard background, was sharp enough, although Kennedy's family had emigrated to America long after the Nixons arrived there. Kennedy, striving to be the first Catholic President, was from one point of view as much an underdog as Nixon.

The ideological difference stressed by Nixon obviously meant a lot to him then and afterwards. 'Kennedy', he says, 'preached the orthodox Democratic gospel of government activism.... I carried the banner of constructive postwar Republicanism, bred of conservative beliefs that a healthy private sector and individual initiative set the best pace for prosperity and progress.' In fact, however, Joe Kennedy's son was unlikely to prove himself an enemy to capitalist values, and when he became President he proved himself an economic conservative.

Nevertheless, the election at the time could fairly be seen as a head-on encounter between the conservative and the progressive. Nixon goes on to say, 'The way the Kennedys played politics and the way the media let them get away with it left me angry and frustrated.' It is to be noted that here and elsewhere he denounces the methods of the Kennedys rather than blaming Jack Kennedy himself. He always liked Jack Kennedy, whose remarks about him were much less generous. The Kennedys by common admission played it rough. In Nixon's eyes it was they who set the standard and he who followed their example in later years.

What is beyond argument is that the media were much more favourable to Kennedy than to Nixon. This could be put down to at least three causes: their liberal preferences; their special hostility to Nixon from the Hiss case onwards; and the unique charisma of Jack Kennedy with which, in his short life, he charmed the whole world. It is no reflection on Nixon to say that in *that* competition neither he nor any other politician of the time would have had a chance.

Nixon in his usual dispassionate way summed up the advantages possessed by each of the rivals. His greatest asset since the attempt to lynch him in Caracas and his confrontation with Khrushchev was the fact that he was probably the best-known figure in the country after Eisenhower. The public also rightly appreciated his vastly greater experience. On the other hand, Kennedy had the immense wealth of his family behind him and what Nixon calls today 'the appeal of his personal style' – in other words, his charisma. But the ultimate handicap under which any Republican candidate laboured was the simple arithmetical fact that there were 50 million Americans of voting age who considered themselves Democrats and only 33 million who considered themselves Republicans. Except for Eisenhower, who carried the Republicans to success as a man above both parties, the Republicans had not had a President since 1932. They were now at their lowest ebb for over thirty years.

Yet there was the unfathomable question of how Kennedy's religion would affect the outcome. No Catholic had ever before been elected President. Did that make it less likely that one would be this time? Nixon still argues that Kennedy's religion, exploited astutely, was of positive advantage to him in the final reckoning. Most good judges appear to take the opposite view, but William Shannon, the present United States Ambassador to Ireland, agrees on balance with Nixon.

The details of the campaign fought with enormous energy on both sides need not detain us now. On one topic, however, Nixon, on the only occasion in his comprehensive memoirs, appears to contradict himself. It has often been said that Kennedy won the election 'on television' and Nixon seems, in certain passages, to support that view. It was agreed by all at the time that Kennedy won a great advantage in the first of the four television debates. Nixon seems to have had the 'edge' among those who only heard the programme on radio (one-fifth of those who saw it on television), which suggests that it was the physical appearance of Kennedy which won the day. Nixon does not deny that his own appearance in the first debate was regrettable: even his mother rang afterwards to ask if he was ill. Recent illness was indeed a main explanation. He corrected matters the next time with the help of make-up. The reference to his 'five o'clock shadow' seems to be rather exaggerated. But Nixon suggests elsewhere in his account that the debates had little significant effect on the outcome of the election, and he produces figures from the public opinion polls in support. So the question whether television did not much affect the result has not been finally decided.

It was touch and go to the end. Eisenhower, brought in towards the end of the campaign, was immensely effective, but Nixon was warned that undue exertion on Eisenhower's part would be fatal to the man in his current state of health. The result was the closest since 1888: Kennedy received 34,221,000 votes and Nixon received 34,108,000 – a difference of only 113,000.

The argument still rages as to whether Kennedy 'really' won and whether Nixon 'really' lost. There is little doubt that there was substantial 'vote fraud' favouring the Democrats, especially in Texas and Illinois. There is the seemingly authentic story of Kennedy ringing Mayor Daley on election night to find out how things were going in Chicago. 'Mr President', said Daley, 'with a little bit of luck and with the help of a few close friends, you are going to carry Illinois.' And Daley saw to it that Kennedy did.

Goldwater is extremely definite about the Democratic malpractices. He gives chapter and verse to prove that Nixon was cheated out of an election victory. And any one who has read his memoirs will realize that he is by no means an undiluted admirer of Nixon. Who knows, however, what would have been the result of a prolonged examination? In any case, Nixon would have none of it. The damage to the United States, the use that would be made of it by the Soviet Union, was sufficient in his eyes to rule out the demand for a recount, which many of his supporters pressed on him. His patriotism here was transparent and even his bitterest critics have seldom questioned it.

He did not concede defeat readily, for which he was criticized by the Kennedy entourage, but not by Jack Kennedy. When it was inevitable, he behaved with proper dignity. He was left with nothing with which to reproach himself. His prestige in no way had been diminished. But his future was now shrouded in total uncertainty. He went to take one last look from the balcony of the White House that looks out across the west grounds of the Capitol. His eyes and mind dwelt on the Washington Monument and the Lincoln Memorial. Now he would be leaving Washington, his home since he had arrived as a young Congressman in 1947. Suddenly he was struck by the thought that this was not the end. 'Some day I would be back here again.'

3
From Nadir to Zenith
1961–8

Nixon, by the time he came to assume presidential office, felt 'prepared', if not quite in the sense of Churchill who in 1940 had felt that all his life had 'prepared him' for this supreme moment. The wilderness years (1961–8) had been 'years of education and growth'. It is likely that a man of fifty-six will be wiser than one of forty-eight. That apart, Nixon was a more mature human being and more of a potential statesman by the time he returned to the White House than when he left it as Vice-President eight years earlier.

In 1970 appeared *The Resurrection of Richard Nixon* by Witcover, still fascinating to anyone interested in Nixon's development. Witcover as he proceeds tends consciously or unconsciously to treat Nixon's actions as governed *entirely* by self-interest and by dedication to his ultimate purpose of being elected as president. This could be said (unfairly) of anyone seeking the highest office in any country, most of all in the United States with its vast electorate and plethora of candidates. Witcover would do well to recall what was said many years ago by Prince von Bülow, the German Chancellor, that 'real statesmen are animated by two motives only, love of country and love of power'. Friends find it easy to see only the first in a politician's career, enemies only the second. It is the duty of the dispassionate historian to strike a balance.

There are, however, reflective passages in Witcover which

35

come close to a true interpretation of Nixon's purposes. He pays a high tribute to Nixon's exceptional powers of self-analysis and, by implication, self-improvement. And he concludes: 'Nixon learned to master himself and when his second chance at the presidency finally came, he was ready. No one', says Witcover, 'will understand how Nixon fashioned his "unprecedented come-back" unless they look at the man as the consummate political creature and at the struggle he waged with the Richard Nixon who had been a loser – and won.' But we will come back to that issue in a moment.

Nixon was not well placed financially in 1961 after fourteen years in politics. Both he and Pat were anxious to return to California in any case. He decided therefore to accept an offer from the Los Angeles law firm of Adams, Duque and Hazeltine. He and his family began to adjust to the new life and to enjoy it, but he was still the nominal head of the Republican Party and at this point was certainly not setting aside political ambitions. He was not left out of things for long. Soon he was being called to the White House by Kennedy for consultation at the time of the Bay of Pigs fiasco. Asked for his opinion, Nixon gave a 'hard line' answer. He told Kennedy, 'I would find a proper legal cover and I would go in ... the most important thing at this point is that we do whatever is necessary to get Castro and communism out of Cuba.' But Kennedy told him that such a policy was not feasible. Nixon spoke out in public in fairly critical terms of Kennedy's handling of the crisis. He found himself emerging without effort on his part as a natural leader of the 'loyal opposition'.

Soon he was under pressure to run for Governor of California in 1962. Much conflicting advice was given him. Eisenhower was strongly in favour of his running – and then aiming at the presidency in 1964. The experts mostly told him: 'Either you run or you have no future in national politics.' Pat, on the other hand, was strongly *against* his running. She argued that she and Richard owed it to Tricia and Julie to spend more time with them during their adolescent years. She herself had no desire whatever to be a celebrity and not much more to be the wife of one. In a family conclave his daughter Tricia (then aged fifteen) came out positively *for* his running. 'I kind of have the feeling that you should run just to show them you are not finished because of the election that was stolen from us in 1960.'

When Nixon announced that he *would* be running for Governor of California in 1962, he said at the same time that he would *not* be running for the presidency in 1964. This was not believed by everyone then or later, but it seems to have been the literal truth at the time.

When the 1962 California election came along, Nixon was on a losing ticket from the start. Whatever chance he had was destroyed by Kennedy's triumph in the Cuba missiles crisis at the end of October 1962. He had to play through to the end what he calls 'the dreary drama'. His defeat was damaging to his fortunes; his manner of accepting it appeared to be fatal.

All night (6/7 November), he sat up in his hotel while the grim news came in on television. In the morning for a long time he refused to come down to meet the Press, but goaded unbearably by the insulting tone of the reporters as he watched them on television, he suddenly announced, 'I am going down there.' It was ten o'clock, but he had not found time to shave: 'I felt terrible, I looked worse.'

In his memoirs he puts the best face he can on the remarks he addressed to the journalists, to their intense amazement. In the fuller text supplied by Witcover, it really does seem that for once his usual self-control had deserted him. There is room for only one quotation, which he gives himself: 'You won't have Nixon to kick around any more because, gentlemen, this is my last Press conference.' He admits that his main press adviser, Herb Klein, was 'shocked and disappointed'. He turned to Herb and said, 'Herb, I did that for you. These guys deserved it and I am glad I did it.' Nixon still sticks to this last sentiment. 'I have never regretted', he writes 'what I said at the "last Press conference".' He insists that he received fairer treatment thereafter from the media for several years. This indeed seems to have been so. At the time he certainly received thousands of favourable letters and telegrams. But whether or not he was wise to lambast the press, it is hardly credible that he would have talked of this being his *last* press conference if he had been in full possession of himself. In other words, he had had a lot of unfair treatment and he 'blew his top'. *Time* magazine was typical of the general comment when it pronounced, 'Barring a miracle, Nixon's public career has ended.'

The fact that the miracle did occur and that Nixon was President of the United States six years later provides the title and the theme of Witcover's book.

No one will ever know, perhaps Nixon himself will never know, how far at that bitter moment he abandoned hope of ever being President, or ever holding high political office again. But his close friend of that time, Murray Chotiner, said much later that 'he felt he was through with politics not by choice but by design. He felt his political career was over.' However, that would seem to refer to politics in the narrower sense. Although he renounced the hope of high office, Nixon surely never intended to get out of politics altogether. Politics in one form or another was meat and drink to him as the law never was. In 1978 I myself, presiding over the lunch already described, heard him answering quite sharp questions with infinite gusto. I noted the sheer enjoyment of his participation in the whole exercise, happy to be back in the world where he was so thoroughly at home.

Non-politicians appreciate quite well the competitive side of politics and no one except possibly Jack Kennedy was ever a keener political competitor than Nixon. But non-politicians seldom realize the fraternity of political life, still less the joy of service it offers, even when the service is only rendered to a political party. No politician could sustain, as Nixon did, the confidence of millions of his fellow citizens over a period of years if he had seemed to them mainly selfish. For the moment, however, we must see him as knocked out of the ring and counted out well and truly.

Soon after his election the defeated Nixon moved himself and his family right across the continent, this time to New York. He was persuaded by his old friend Elmer Bobst, chairman of a major pharmaceutical company, that nothing now tied him to California, that business opportunities would be much greater in New York and that life there would be much more interesting and stimulating. Pat and the girls were disenchanted with California after the election and were quite excited by the prospect of living in New York. Pat indeed had an extra reason for preferring it. 'She felt strongly that now was the time for me to get out of the political arena once and for all.'

Nixon still believes that, by moving to New York where Nelson Rockefeller was supreme, he was deliberately ruling himself out as an active political figure for the foreseeable future. But who knows what aspirations were left at the back of his mind?

Nixon set off in June for a six-week holiday in Europe and the Middle East. Throughout these years we must think of him as steadily enhancing his prestige as an international expert by regular travel and impressive high-level contacts. By autumn 1963 he was beginning to be besieged from all over the country with demands that he should be the Republican presidential candidate in 1964. Whether there are any circumstances in which he would have accepted nomination is a moot question. There is no sign that he ever lifted a finger to secure it. The Republican candidate who emerged was Barry Goldwater, a right-wing ultra-patriotic figure generally described today as an extreme reactionary. (On this and other points he is thoroughly entertaining in his own memoirs.) Nixon was no admirer of Goldwater's policies, though he liked him very much as a man, as indeed did everyone who knew him well. When the election came Nixon worked unstintingly in what he certainly knew was a hopeless cause. Goldwater was duly overwhelmed by Johnson.

But meanwhile the tragedy of President Kennedy's assassination had shaken the world. Nixon had always liked Kennedy, admired him and perhaps envied his possession of certain graces to which Nixon could not lay claim. His letter to Kennedy's widow and hers to him ought to be read in full. Only these extracts can be given. After paying tribute to the late President, Nixon went on, 'But I want you to know that the nation will also be forever grateful for your service as First Lady. You brought to the White House charm, beauty and elegance as the official hostess for America and the mystique of the young in heart which was uniquely yours made an indelible impression on the American consciousness.' Her letter to him contained this passage: 'Just one thing I would say to you – if it does not work out as you have hoped for so long – please be consoled by what you already have – your life and

your family. We never value life enough when we have it –
and I would not have had Jack live his life any other way –
though I know his death could have been prevented and I
will never cease to torture myself with that.'

The Kennedys and the Nixons had little in common soci-
ally. There was a certain contempt on the Kennedys' side
which is unattractive to read about. But Jackie Kennedy and
Richard Nixon were both capable of true personal feeling and
of entering deeply on occasion into the feelings of others.

On 9 January 1965 Nixon held a small family party to cele-
brate his birthday. He was fifty-two, the same age incidentally
as the Queen of England and the British Prime Minister at
the time of writing. Afterwards he retired to his study; he
looked back over the past year and considered the future. He
had long had a passionate admiration for Churchill. Now he
drew encouragement from the fact that Churchill, in his later
fifties, had refused to write himself off when he was written
off by so many others. Nixon, concerned as always with his
self-improvement, wrote down eight New Year resolutions
for 1965 which, unlike most of us, he intended seriously to
carry out:

  Set great goals
  Daily rest
  Brief vacations
  Knowledge of all weaknesses
  Better use of time
  Begin writing book
  Golf or some other kind of daily exercise
  Articles or speeches on provocative new international and
    national issues.

Not a very original list perhaps, but certainly not an ignoble
one. About this time he began to consider how he should
approach the race for the presidency, if he should decide to
run.

Three and a half years later, on 7 August 1968, he was to
be nominated by overwhelming acclaim as the presidential
candidate at the Republican Convention. The period up till
that date falls naturally into two parts, the first up to the end

of 1966 and from then till August 1968. The first period was to end in a striking success. On the domestic front, he considers, looking back, that the philosophic distinction between Republicans and Democrats was sharper than at any time: Self-help or State action, Thatcherism versus 'Butskellism' in British terms. He was convinced that Johnson's 'great society' was failing to satisfy the immense expectations aroused. He could denounce its weaknesses with complete ideological sincerity.

He was anxious, however, that the Republicans should not become established as a merely negative party. He called on them to be *Lincoln* Republicans with their own brand of idealism. He insisted that the party should have no room for racism; he castigated in that connection black and white extremists (but how did he define them?) with equal vigour. On Vietnam he was genuinely anxious to avoid fractious criticism. But he paid visits to Saigon in 1964 and again in 1965 and came away horrified at the general ineffectiveness. On his return after the latter visit he made pronouncements that can only be described as 'hawkish'.

In March 1965 Johnson had thanked him personally for his public restraint over the Vietnam issue, presenting him indeed with a pair of presidential cuff-links. But the happy relationship temporarily broke down; a fine old row developed during the 1966 congressional elections. In September Johnson made a surprise announcement that he was going to meet with President Nguyen Van Thieu of South Vietnam and other Vietnamese and allied leaders in Manila in late October, just two weeks before the election. In a newspaper column Nixon was writing at this time, he bluntly noted the widespread scepticism that greeted this announcement. He wrote, 'From diplomats in Tokyo to members of the President's own party in Washington, the question is being posed: Is this a quest for peace or a quest for votes?'

The acrimony increased. Johnson spoke with unparalleled severity about a former Vice-President. 'I do not', he said, 'want to get into a debate on a foreign policy meeting in Manila with a chronic campaigner like Mr Nixon. It is his problem to find fault with his country and with his government during a period of October every two years. You will

41

remember what President Eisenhower said – that if you would give him a week or so, he would figure out what he was doing.' (President Eisenhower frequently apologized to Nixon for that unhappy comment.)

Nixon now saw his chance of playing a dignified role as the injured party. His reply to Johnson finished with the innocent-sounding suggestion: 'Let us be gentlemen about this and have our discussions in a reasonable way.' Nixon suddenly found himself the centre of national attention and at last began to get a positively 'good Press'.

Witcover spent a week with Nixon as the only reporter on a 'swing' through the Mid-West, South-West and South in June 1966. Every now and then there had been a so-called 'new Nixon', but this 'new, new Nixon' was a revelation to Witcover. 'It was an instant education', he writes, 'for any Nixon doubter. For all his obviousness, for all his forced gaiety, for all his apple pie Americanism he entertained audience after audience. He held their attention and finally he roused them.' By this time he was well aware that he was accused of deviousness, was nick-named 'Tricky Dicky' or 'Dick the Trick'. He seemed determined to grasp the nettle of this accusation by extra candour. Witcover thought that he carried this a little far at times in explaining his various methods for dealing with different audiences. But by and large the impression left on Witcover was of a man well aware of his main weaknesses and going far to overcome them.

The election of 1966 was the best result the Republicans had had for many a year. They exceeded even Nixon's expectations, winning a net 47 House seats, 3 Senate seats, 8 governorships and 540 seats in the State legislature. Nixon had played a major part in the Republican triumph, which boded well for his own return to the heights.

Now he took a rather surprising step. He wanted to leave open till the last possible moment the decision whether he would or would not actually run for President in 1968. He announced that he would take a six-month moratorium from party politics and travel abroad. In fact he made four major trips: to Europe and the Soviet Union, to Latin America, to Asia and to Africa and the Middle East. He met the leaders in almost all cases and as many ordinary people as possible. When he returned he made a major speech in July 1967 at the Bohemian Grove, the site of the annual summer retreat of San Francisco's prestigious Bohemian Club, and published a comprehensive article on foreign affairs in October.

The Bohemian Grove speech he refers to as the one that gave him most pleasure and satisfaction in his whole political career. There is only room for one passage here:

As we enter this last third of the twentieth century the hopes of the world rest with America. Whether peace and freedom survive in the world depends on American leadership.

Never has a nation had more advantages to lead. Our economic superiority is enormous; our military superiority can be whatever we choose to make it. Most important, it happens that we are on the right side – the side of freedom and peace and progress against the forces of totalitarianism, reaction and war.

There is only one area where there is any question – that is whether America has the national character and moral stamina to see us through this long and difficult struggle.

In his foreign affairs article he had a good deal to say about China of much significance in view of later developments. Here again one can only quote a single passage:

For the short run then, this means a policy of firm restraint, of no reward, of a creative counterpressure designed to persuade Peking that its interests can be served only by accepting the basic rules of international civility. For the long run, it means pulling China back into the world community – but as a great and progressing nation, not as the epicenter of world revolution.

On 30 September a message reached him from his brother that his mother had just died. She had suffered a stroke two years earlier. Whenever Nixon was in the Los Angeles area he drove out to see her. 'She never gave any signs of awareness and could speak only in monosyllables, but I felt sure that in the deep recesses of her mind she recognized me.' The last time that Richard had talked to her before her stroke she had just had an operation and was in terrible pain, although she never once complained about it. All he could say was, 'Mother, don't give up.' She pulled herself up in bed and said with sudden strength, 'Richard, don't *you* give up. Don't let

43

anybody tell *you* you are through.' 'A marvellous legacy' is how he described his debt to her. This supreme duty of not giving up, not quitting, was to remain very deep in him. Without understanding this, one cannot enter into his mind in his last year at the White House.

Nixon tells us that even at the end of December 1967 he was still not quite certain that he wished to stand for the presidency. Somehow one feels that his decision had already been taken. Much time is spent by excellent writers like Witcover in discussing the strategy and tactics which resulted in Nixon becoming the official Republican candidate a year or so after his moratorium ended. In retrospect it all looks rather simple. Governor George Romney of Michigan was for some time the front runner; a delightful man, deeply religious, refusing to practise politics on a Sunday, yet extremely successful as a business man. A hero in Michigan, but a child in the world of national politics, he was easily turned to ridicule by the media. It was not long before he destroyed himself by his ineptitude in answering questions on Vietnam. After that it was hardly possible that Nixon should fail to secure the Republican nomination.

At the time, however, his 'loser' image was considered a terrible handicap, even by the Republican activists who were truly grateful to him for his unceasing labours over so many years on their behalf. Nixon reached the conclusion, obvious it now seems, that to shed the 'loser' image he must win something important. He must enter the primaries in 1968. This he did with spectacular success.

Theodore White describes the impression made on him by the new Nixon at this time: 'By the late spring of 1968 my reportorial observation on Nixon had deeply changed from that of 1960 – chiefly because he had changed too. There was in all he said, even in discussing the most hostile personalities, a total absence of bitterness, of the rancour and venom that had once coloured his remarks. I had learned, as I had not known before, how diligent and untiring a worker he was – and how phenomenally driven to get to the bottom of things. ....'

By this time Nixon had collected round him some remarkable men, fully the equals for electoral and, in some cases, for wider purposes of those who promoted Kennedy in 1960. The speech writers Ray Price, Pat Buchanan and Bill Safire were each brilliant in his own way. The overall manager was Bob Haldeman, dedicated to Nixon since 1956. His public relations background was his immediate strength and his ultimate limitation.

In the history of the United States the most traumatic events in the first half of 1968 did not directly concern Nixon, though they were to affect his fortunes profoundly. The ever greater and more violent hostility to the Vietnam War was the background to everything. There was the emergence of Eugene McCarthy as a 'peace in Vietnam' candidate; the eventual decision of Bobby Kennedy to raise the same standard with much greater resources behind him; the staggering announcement from President Johnson that he was not going to run again; finally the assassination of Bobby Kennedy.

When the dust settled, Hubert Humphrey emerged as the Democratic candidate. At that time Vice-President – a former Senator of much experience, no mean orator, though inclined to verbosity – he was liked by all, if not renowned for his strength or dynamism, and arguably the nicest man in American politics. Nixon had prepared his own campaign independently of any Democratic comings and goings, though bearing in mind the increasing unpopularity of President Johnson who had won such a staggering triumph less than four years before.

We return to 'Teddy' White for a just reappraisal:

If there was a confidence, vigor and new self-restraint in Nixon-on-the-stump of 1968, the Nixon-at-work in 1968 was even more greatly changed. Few campaigns had been more badly mismanaged than the Nixon campaign of 1960, with its overlapping and conflicting authorities,... its bottlenecks choking every access to his decision at every stage. The new campaign of 1968 reflected much that Nixon had learned since 1960, a capacity for growth undeniable.

On policy, the course Nixon had set himself was quite clear: 'peace abroad, peace at home, an end to adventure, unity in the party, unity in the nation'. In March he had committed himself rather unguardedly to what was understood to be a pledge that if he were elected the war with Vietnam would soon be brought to an end. But on the whole he had been able to avoid explaining how he would bring this about. He had managed to present himself as too responsible a statesman to interfere with the President's attempts at peace-making.

In September the result seemed cut and dried. At the end of that month a Gallup Poll reported Nixon 15 points ahead of Humphrey, with 43 to his 28 (and Wallace the ultra-conservative more-or-less-racialist candidate with 21). But then at last Hubert Humphrey set aside his advisors and spoke from the heart. Suddenly he came out with a more or less unconditional call to end the bombing in Vietnam and in a flash his fortunes improved dramatically. By mid-October he was within 5 points of Nixon and gaining steadily. There was little that Nixon could do in response; he continued on his statesmanlike and cautious way.

Then a still larger bombshell was dropped by Lyndon Johnson. Quite unexpectedly he telephoned Nixon (also the other candidates Humphrey and Wallace). There had been a breakthrough in Paris, he said, and after wide consultations among his advisers, he had decided to call a total bombing halt in Vietnam. As Johnson went on, Nixon thought to himself, 'Whatever this means to North Vietnam he has just dropped a pretty good bomb in the middle of my campaign.' Johnson insisted that he was not concerned with the election. That was hard for Nixon to swallow. But he did the correct thing and promised support in public. Soon it emerged that President Thieu and his government would not participate in the negotiations Johnson was proposing. Nixon authorized his intimate advisor Bob Finch to point out to the press that the prospects for peace were not as advanced as Johnson's announcement might have made them seem. Off the record Finch explained, 'We had the impression that all the diplomatic ducks were in position.' On the record, he said, 'I think this will boomerang. It was hastily contrived.'

Johnson was predictably furious. It was suggested that Nixon might telephone him to calm him down. When he did so Johnson demanded, 'Who is this guy Fink? Why is he taking out after me?' Nixon said, 'Mr President, that is Finch, not Fink.' Johnson continued to refer to him as Fink. Eventually some kind of amity was restored. But there is no doubt that Johnson's last-minute intervention, however motivated, was of much assistance to Humphrey and damage to Nixon.

The gap narrowed and narrowed again. Nixon realized on election night that he was in for another cliff-hanger, though he still felt fairly confident of winning. He put his family in a separate suite on the thirty-fifth floor of the Waldorf Towers in New York. Always considerate to them, he did not want to make them feel that they had to keep up a cheerful front for his sake. At 10.30 pm the national results were still the same – Humphrey and Nixon neck and neck. It was not till 8.30 in the morning that Nixon's young aide, Dwight Chapin, rushed in shouting, 'You've got it; you've won!' No one had become closer to Nixon than John Mitchell, his law partner and closest friend in politics. Nixon put his hand on John Mitchell's shoulder: 'Well, John, we had better get down to Florida and get this thing planned out.' Tears welled up in Mitchell's eyes. 'Mr President', he said quietly, 'I think I had better go up to be with Martha.' Martha, his wife, had been in a rest home during the last weeks of the campaign. The emotional strain imposed on Mitchell by her nervous temperament was to have tragic effects later on.

Nixon sat alone with Pat, who had suffered agonies during the night. When he told her it was all over she asked emotionally, remembering all too well the way in which Illinois was 'stolen' in 1960: 'Dick, are we sure of Illinois? Are we completely sure?' Richard Nixon told her that they were sure of victory beyond any possibility of reversal. She burst into tears of relief and joy.

Humphrey as gracious in defeat as he had been tenacious in combat conceded Nixon's victory. Nixon with his family went down to the ballroom of the Waldorf Astoria where hundreds of supporters had kept the all-night vigil. He told them of Humphrey's call and how well he knew what it was like to lose a 'close one'. He could not help adding, 'Winning's a lot more fun.' He told an anecdote of the campaign when a teenager had held up a sign reading: 'Bring Us Together.' 'That', said Nixon, 'will be the great objective of our administration at the outset, to bring the American people together.'

4
The Global Vision
1969

Nixon was inaugurated President of the United States on 20 January 1969. Pat held the same two Milhous family bibles which she had held in 1953 and 1967. They were opened at Richard's request at Isaiah 2,4: 'They shall beat their swords into ploughshares and their spears into pruning hooks: nation shall not lift up sword against nation, neither shall they learn war any more.' His major theme was peace. 'The greatest honour', he said, 'that history can bestow is the title of peacemaker. This honour now beckons America...'

Chuck Colson, Nixon's counsel from 1969 to 1972 and for some time as close to Nixon as anyone, told me recently that the depth of Nixon's passion for peace was never fully understood.

I recall that in the 1930s Anthony Eden, then the rising star of British politics and an outstanding champion of the League of Nations, was described by a French statesman as 'this terrible young man with his passion for peace'. Anthony Eden drew his inspiration from his experience as a front-line soldier in the First World War; Nixon, though also a war veteran, drew his from his Quaker upbringing, but the effect on the man was the same. There was nothing woolly about Nixon's peace-loving vision. No American President can ever have been so well-equipped, on taking office for the first time, with sheer knowledge of foreign countries. Certainly none of them ever approached more systematically the task of framing a far-reaching international policy.

Nixon came to his task highly dissatisfied with American foreign policy during the 1960s. The tendency to become preoccupied with only one or two problems at a time had led to deterioration of policy on all fronts. He did not feel that there should be any single foreign policy priority. There were many priorities, each affecting the others, but he would have to start somewhere. He put Europe at the top of the list. NATO was in disarray, largely because of the failure of the United States to consult adequately with European allies. He had plans for dealing with the Far East and the Middle East, but the central factor on the eve of his presidency was the same in his eyes as it had been in 1947 when he went to Europe with the Herter Committee.

'America, now as then, was the main defender of the free world against the encroachment and aggression of the communist world.' He had never doubted, and still does not doubt, that the communists meant it when they said that their goal was to bring the world under communist control. But unlike some anti-communists he had always believed or, at any rate, believed by this time that the West could and must communicate, and when possible negotiate with communist nations.

In his new book *The Real War* (1980) Nixon spells out his current thinking about the communist menace and the way to deal with it, in the interests of world peace. His basic ideas of today were present in embryo in 1969. 'What threatens the world,' he writes, 'is not theoretical communism, not philosophical Marxism, it is rather an aggressive, expansionist totalitarian force that has adopted those names but grafted its own ideological fervour on to the roots of tsarist expansionism and tsarist despotism.' But he emphasizes that today's version of the ever-expanding Russian empire, the Soviet Union, has been made different from the old empire by the intense missionary zeal, the ideological fervour of communism itself – of Marxism as reinterpreted by Lenin and his heirs. These provide 'a rationale for tyranny', a banner under which to rally the desperate or the discontented. People in other countries who would not lay down their lives for a tsar would risk all for the promises, however false, held out by the prophets of communism.

Again, what he has to say today about détente must be read into the policy he attempted to operate as President. He says that we should think of détente as a complement to containment, not as a substitute for it. 'Containment, the task of resisting Russian expansionism, has been and must remain the *sine qua non* of any United States foreign policy. Détente is an attempt to avoid possible fatal miscalculation, to reduce differences where possible through negotiations and to provide possible incentives for the Russians and the Chinese to co-operate with the United States in maintaining a stable world order.' In 1969 it was, as it is today, the only policy that makes sense in the nuclear age.

We shall be coming to Henry Kissinger in a moment. Something he writes in his memoirs (1979) in relation to the Moscow summit of 1972 sums up what Nixon with his help was striving for throughout his presidency. 'For as far ahead as we can see, America's task will be to re-create the two pillars of our policy towards the Soviet Union; a willingness to confront Soviet expansionism and a simultaneous readiness to mark out a co-operative future.'

Meanwhile the Soviets had been making rapid progress in the Arab states, in Cuba and in North Vietnam, where they had supplanted the Chinese as the principal military suppliers. Militarily they were far stronger in relation to the United States than five years earlier, though the full extent of their military development was much under-estimated by the CIA. The picture was not altogether unfavourable. The Soviet split with China, steadily developing during the 1960s, was profoundly significant. China was beginning to see the USSR rather than the United States as its principal enemy. There was the possibility of a totally new relationship with China herself.

What, however, Kissinger calls the most pressing foreign problem was the war in Vietnam, where Johnson had left behind him half a million American troops with no prospect whatever of an early end to the war. Nixon had been cagey – some would say almost too clever – in his handling of this problem up until his election. He had talked in March 1968

Richard Nixon aged three (standing on the right) with his parents and two of his brothers.

Richard Nixon aged twelve (second from left) with his three brothers.

Vice-President Nixon with his wife Pat and daughters Patricia (on the left) and Julie.

The Inauguration of Richard Nixon as 37th President of the United States, 20 January 1969.

President Nixon
expounds his views to
three devoted aides in
the famous Oval Office
in the White House.
From left to right:
Robert Haldeman,
Dwight Chapin and
John Ehrlichman.

President Nixon is
welcomed by US
troops on his visit to
Vietnam in 1969.

President Nixon is entertained to lunch at Chequers by the Queen and Mr Heath on his visit to England in October 1970.

The President with his wife and family photographed in the White House under a portrait of George Washington. Standing left to right: David Eisenhower, grandson of the late President Eisenhower and the husband of Julie Nixon (seated left), Richard Nixon, Pat Nixon and Edward Cox, husband of Tricia (seated right).

Two historic handshakes: *Above* Richard Nixon is greeted by
Chou-En-lai on his arrival at Peking Airport in February 1972.
Below Nixon with Chairman Mao.

Richard and Pat Nixon on the Great Wall of China.

Richard Nixon consults with Henry Kissinger in the confines of the Kremlin on their way to the conference table.

The nuclear arms agreement is signed with Russia, 21 June 1973.

President Nixon
addresses the nation
about the Watergate
cover-up less than a
week before his
resignation.

The Nixons in
retirement in
California.

of an early end to the war. Everyone for one reason or another was in favour of an early finish to it.

But the two simple ways of ending it were both, in fact, inadmissible. The domestic and international uproar that would have accompanied the use of any of the available knock-out blows would have made such a policy impossible to carry through. On the other hand, a precipitate withdrawal would leave American prisoners in the hands of the enemy and abandon seventeen million South Vietnamese to communist atrocities and domination. Once a quick military victory was ruled out, the only possible course was to try for a fair negotiated settlement that would preserve the independence of South Vietnam and secure the return of the prisoners.

In *The Real War* Nixon informs us that his goals in Vietnam when he took office in 1969 were as follows:

(1) Build up the South Vietnamese armed forces.

(2) Strengthen the economy.

(3) Help the South Vietnamese extend their control over the countryside.

(4) Reduce the invasion threat by destroying enemy sanctuaries and supply lines in Cambodia and Laos.

(5) Withdraw the half million American troops from Vietnam in a way that would not bring about a collapse in the south.

(6) Negotiate a cease-fire and a peace treaty.

(7) Demonstrate our willingness and determination to stand by our ally if the peace agreement was violated by Hanoi, and assure South Vietnam that it would continue to receive our military aid as Hanoi did from its allies, the Soviet Union and to a lesser extent China.

These aims had to be pursued not in some world of abstract conception, but against the background of American public opinion. One of the most valuable services rendered by Kissinger's memoirs already referred to is the emphasis laid on the absolute necessity of carrying the American public along, if any real success was to be achieved. Inevitably, in anything that Nixon writes on the subject, it is tempting to find a personal motive. But Kissinger can discuss the whole issue more objectively.

Nixon was prepared to take most of his first year in office to arrive at a negotiated agreement. In the event it took four years and overran the 1972 election. And the long delay was very damaging in the adverse effect on American public opinion. Yet when the time came for settlement, Nixon could claim, with some justification, that his objectives had been achieved, although he was aware that the peace was extremely fragile. In later years he could blame Congress with still more justification for withdrawing aid to South Vietnam soon afterwards, and thereby sabotaging their chance of continued independence. In the end all that was saved were the American prisoners-of-war. But they at least showed him in a dark hour profound gratitude on their return home.

When I was writing a life of John Kennedy, published in 1976, I was astonished to find how little thought he appeared to have given to the policies he would be pursuing after victory. He gave no thought at all, it would seem, in advance to the selection of his chief Cabinet ministers. Of the three most important, Kennedy had never met two before, and the third was a member of the previous Republican administration. Nixon cannot be faulted in this way, though the comparison is unfair. Kennedy was, relatively speaking, a novice aged forty-three. Nixon, aged fifty-six, by this time had twice been Vice-President.

But his plans for a Cabinet of all the talents with bi-partisan representation soon ran into difficulties. His defeated opponent, Hubert Humphrey, turned down the United Nations ambassadorship; so did President Kennedy's brother-in-law, Sargent Schriver, rather, it would seem, reluctantly. Another Democrat, Senator Henry Jackson of Washington, turned down an offer to be Secretary of Defence. Nixon tried to obtain some black leaders as members of his administration but here again he was rebuffed.

Still, he was able to collect round him some notable men, of whom Bill Rogers, 'a strong administrator', would have the 'formidable job of managing the recalcitrant bureaucracy of the State Department'. He was a close personal friend of Nixon, as was the powerful, rather enigmatic John Mitchell, Nixon's law partner who became Attorney-General. 'I counted him', says Nixon, 'my most trusted friend and adviser, and I wanted to have his advice available not just on legal matters, but on the whole range of presidential decision-making.' The other appointments were fairly straightforward, except that they included two dazzling Harvard professors. They both put me in mind of Dick Crossman, though the differences are as patent as the similarities.

'Daniel Patrick Moynihan', writes Nixon, 'had helped design the Great Society poverty programs, but he was not afraid to acknowledge that many of them had failed, and he was ready to apply the lessons learned from that failure to devising new programs that might work.' Later on, as American representative at the United Nations, he was to make a memorable stand on behalf of human rights. But in the period of the Nixon presidency, it was the other professor who gained the chief glory.

Henry Kissinger, after a Bavarian Jewish childhood, had fled from the Nazis at the age of fifteen, served in American Army counter-intelligence in the Second World War, and achieved resounding academic success at Harvard. His patron in the years before 1968 was Nelson Rockefeller, defeated by Nixon for the Republican nomination, at which point Kissinger, who had never concealed his low opinion of Nixon, commented, 'I could never vote for Nixon, of course.' He called Nixon publicly 'the most dangerous of the candidates'. He was astonished to be asked by Nixon to become his National Security Adviser. He gives, incidentally, an arresting picture of his first reception by Nixon. 'His manner was almost diffident; his movements were slightly vague and unrelated to what he was saying, as if two different impulses were behind speech and gesture. He spoke in a low gentle voice. While he talked he sipped one after another cups of coffee that were brought in without his asking for them.' At the end of the conversation Kissinger told the President-elect that he would be of no use to him 'without the moral support of his friends and associates', a judgement that Kissinger disarmingly admits proved to be false. Kissinger asked for a week to consult these friends and associates.

'This extraordinary request', comments Kissinger, still

more disarmingly, reflected to no small extent the insularity of the academic profession and the arrogance of the Harvard faculty. Nixon was often to be accused of paranoia, but this little anecdote shows that he had something to be paranoiac about in the attitude of the eastern liberal establishment. In the end Kissinger said that he would be proud to accept. The eastern liberal establishment seemed to be relieved. Arthur Schlesinger described the appointment as 'excellent, very encouraging'. They were glad to have their man on the inside, though later on they smiled on the other side of their faces.

Members of the Nixon entourage have not been kind on the whole in what they have written about Kissinger, though ready to describe him as a most entertaining companion. In these accounts he showed himself on occasion a hawk in the office and a dove by the time he reached the liberal circuit in Washington. William Shawcross in his book *Sideshow* (a tremendous diatribe against Nixon and Kissinger), tells a risible story of Kissinger assuring Nixon after his 1976 visit to China that he had been 'very, very clever', and then mocking him to Nelson Rockefeller.

Kissinger himself admits to an episode in which he says 'I take no great pride'. At the end of 1972 the word got about that he had opposed the heavy bombing of North Vietnam carried out on Nixon's orders. He admits that he did little to dampen the speculation and that 'Nixon was justifiably infuriated by the assertion by columnists that I had opposed the bombing. Though our relationship remained professional in the inevitable daily contacts between security adviser and President, there were many telltale signs of presidential disfavour.'

By this time there was what Kissinger calls 'a painful rift' between himself and Nixon. Nevertheless, they soldiered on together and at the very end of his presidency Nixon was treating him as his most intimate friend in public life. Their partnership was immensely fruitful. Kissinger still believes that if the executive power of the presidency had not been destroyed by Watergate, they would have achieved without qualification their highest purposes.

After I had completed the first draft of this book, I met

Henry Kissinger at a party for the publication of his memoirs. 'What is your assessment of the ex-President?' Dr Kissinger asked me. 'A great man *manqué*,' was all I could manage on the spur of the moment. Dr Kissinger concurred. No doubt he would have expanded on the theme, but the pressure of others desiring to speak to him made further discussion at that point impossible, though we had some conversation later.

The whole idea of appointing a National Security Adviser was bound to cause difficulties with Rogers at the head of the State Department. Nixon refers to these rather blandly: 'Rogers felt that Kissinger was Machiavellian, deceitful, egotistical, arrogant and insulting. Kissinger felt that Rogers was vain, uninformed, unable to keep a secret and hopelessly dominated by the State Department bureaucracy. The problems became increasingly serious as the years passed.'

When Harold Wilson formed his British Cabinet in October 1964, it was optimistically forecast that there would be a creative tension between the Chancellor of the Exchequer, James Callaghan, and the Secretary of State for Economic Affairs, George Brown. It did not work out well, nor did it in Nixon's Cabinet. Kissinger eventually acquired both positions; before that happened, the friction had been painful and damaging.

It is fair to record a somewhat different view from Gerald Ford who, as Minority (Republican) Leader in the Senate, was well placed to judge. He tells us that he was pleased with the men Nixon chose to serve in his Cabinet. Mel Laird would be an excellent Secretary of Defence, George Romney would do well at the Department of Housing and Urban Development and Bill Rogers 'would provide quiet leadership at the Department of State'. The appointment of Henry Kissinger as National Security Adviser to the President was, he thought, a master stroke. He had 'invited me to speak at his Harvard graduate school seminars on several occasions in the past and I had been enormously impressed by his grasp of the nuances of foreign policy'. He did not and does not seem concerned about the inevitable friction between Kissinger and Rogers.

Nixon was to look back on 1969 as a 'solid beginning'. He could reasonably feel that his plans for a new kind of international understanding on the highest level were proceeding according to plan. But in the event he had made no real progress on Vietnam by the end of the year and time was certainly not going to help him. Public opinion statistically might be with him, but protest was becoming more and more violent.

On 17 February the Soviet Ambassador, Anatoly Dobrynin, paid his first official call. Arrangements had already been made for the establishment of a private channel between him and Kissinger. They were to meet once a week, usually for lunch. (What, we may ask, about poor Rogers, the Secretary of State?) The Ambassador told the President that his government would welcome talks on arms limitation. But Nixon stuck firmly to his new principle of linkage.

'History', he said, 'makes it clear that wars result not so much from arms, or even from arms races, as they do from underlying political differences and political problems. So I think it incumbent on us, when we begin strategic arms talks, to do what we can in a parallel way to defuse critical political situations like the Middle East and Vietnam and Berlin, where there is a danger that arms might be put to use.' Before he left the Ambassador handed Nixon an official seven-page note from Moscow which indicated that the Soviets were prepared to move forward on a whole range of topics including the Middle East, Central Europe, Vietnam and arms control. Nixon was encouraged by the interview, though distinctly sceptical as to whether Soviet action would follow words.

Soon (23 February) he set off for Europe, taking in his stride Brussels (the North Atlantic Council), the Queen of England and Prime Minister Harold Wilson, Premier de Gaulle and Pope Paul VI. He was determined to show that America was solidly behind the European nations in their defence against the Soviet menace and genuinely dedicated to NATO. An anecdote of his dinner at Downing Street bears quotation, though admittedly belonging to the *Wit and Wisdom of the Great* variety. The *New Statesman* in 1962 had described Nixon's defeat in California as a 'victory for decency'. The editor at that time was John Freeman, now in 1969 the newly appointed Ambassador to the United States, and meeting Nixon for the first time on this occasion. Nixon decided that frankness was the best kind of delicacy. 'Much worse things', he said, in replying to a toast after dinner, 'have been written about me by American journalists. Let bygones be bygones. After all, John Freeman is the new diplomat and I am the new statesman.' (Loud laughter and applause.) Wilson scribbled on the back of a menu: 'That was one of the kindest and most generous acts I have known in a quarter of a century in politics. You can't guarantee being born a lord. It is possible – you have shown it – to be born a gentleman.' Richard Nixon and Harold Wilson were both good at that kind of thing.

Kissinger adds touches of his own. He tells us that 'the usual imperturbable Freeman was close to tears'. Thus was born a mission to Washington that proved a spectacular success: 'John Freeman was one of the most effective ambassadors I have ever dealt with.' Kissinger also reminds us that Wilson invited Nixon to attend a Cabinet meeting, an unprecedented honour for a foreigner: 'When we first encountered him, Harold Wilson had the reputation of a wily politician whose penetrating intelligence was flawed by the absence of ultimate reliability.... With the United States I always found him a man of his word.'

Nixon was enormously impressed by de Gaulle. His admiration for him approached, without quite equalling, that which he felt for Churchill. De Gaulle said that the central fact of life for post-war Europe was the Soviet threat, but he believed that the Soviets themselves had become preoccupied with China. 'They are thinking in terms of a possible clash with China and they know they cannot fight the West at the same time. Thus I believe that they may end up by opting for a policy of *rapprochement* with the West.' And he added: 'To work towards détente is a matter of good sense; if you are not ready to make war, make peace.' As regards China, he revealed thoughts that were close to those of Nixon. 'I have no illusions', he said, 'about their ideology, but I do not feel that we should leave them isolated in their rage.... It is vital that we have more communications with them than we have today.'

Nixon did not hesitate to ask: 'Mr President, what would you do regarding Vietnam?' De Gaulle replied that the only way to end the war was by conducting negotiations on political and military issues simultaneously and by establishing a calendar for the departure of the American troops. 'I do not believe', he said, 'that you should depart with undue haste.' This advice which sounded rational at the time would not help much, but who was suggesting anything better? Nixon felt that the new *entente cordiale* between the Presidents of France and the United States alone would have made a European trip worthwhile. But de Gaulle did not last long afterwards. He resigned on 28 April as President of France.

Nixon returned home to find Eisenhower approaching his end. By this time, whatever the past ambiguities in their relationship, they had become very close. Richard and Pat had been delighted when, in the previous December, their daughter Julie had married Eisenhower's grandson David. She and her sister Tricia are rightly referred to again and again as remarkable young women, whose loyalty in the darkest days to Richard Nixon edified all beholders.

Bill Safire has written: 'My favourite Nixon has always been Julie Eisenhower. She is like her father without a dark side – that is, she is loyal, alert, considerate, virtuous, intelligent and sensibly impulsive. That may sound like a version of the Girl Scout pledge, but most people who watched her speak up for her father in the worst of times would agree that Julie is not only all that, but is pluckier than any member of her family, including her father, in opening up to people.'

Personally I cannot judge between the two sisters. In my case Tricia holds the advantage having left a moving and vividly written diary from which I will be quoting later.

Nixon saw Eisenhower for the last time two days before he died. Nixon told him, as he said farewell, 'General, I just want you to know how all the free people of Europe and millions of others in the world will for ever be in your debt for the leadership you provided in war and peace. You can always take great pride in the fact that no man in our history has done more to make America and the world a better and safer place in which to live.' Eisenhower lifted his head from the pillow. 'Mr President', he said, 'you do me great honour in what you have just said.' Then 'he slowly raised his hand to his forehead in a final salute'.

Nixon's pen-portrait of Eisenhower throws interesting

light on both of them. 'Eisenhower', he says, 'has a warm smile and icy blue eyes.' This sounds like the perfect description of a *faux bonhomme*, but Nixon goes out of his way to eradicate such an impression. He describes Eisenhower as having an 'exceptional warmth, but there was always a reserve, even an aloofness that balanced it'. Those who knew him best realized that they did not know him really well. Nixon implies that this combination of warmth and personal detachment was essential to Eisenhower's greatness, but not to greatness of all kinds. It did not embody his own aspiration.

In March Nixon, with Kissinger at his elbow, took a step which has been widely criticized and which was certainly carried out in a manner to provoke controversy. In February the North Vietnamese had launched a 'small-scale but savage' offensive into South Vietnam – a test, it seemed, of the new President's resolution. While Nixon was in Europe the attacks intensified. On his return he was soon being pressed to say what reply he intended. He said at one point 'an appropriate response will be made to these attacks if they continue'. On 16 March Nixon held a crucial meeting with Rogers (Secretary of State), Laird (Secretary for Defence), Kissinger and General Wheeler, the Chairman of the Joint Chiefs of Staff. American casualties were heavy under the impact of the communist offensive. Intelligence reports indicated that over 40,000 communist troops had been amassed secretly in the zone ten to fifteen miles wide just inside the Cambodian border. Cambodia was a neutral country. The United States respected that neutrality, but the communists were blatantly violating it by launching raids across the Cambodian border into South Vietnam and then retreating to the safety of their jungle sanctuaries. The United States were well within their legal rights in refusing to allow this to continue.

'Gentlemen', said Nixon, 'we have reached the point where a decision is required – to bomb or not to bomb.' The decision to bomb was duly taken. Recently, William Shawcross, as already mentioned, has produced a tremendous denunciation of Nixon and Kissinger in his deeply felt book *Sideshow*. 'In Cambodia', he says, 'imperatives of a small and vulnerable people were consciously sacrificed to the interests of strategic design. Cambodia was not a mistake. It was a crime.' And in his account Nixon and Kissinger are the criminals. William Shawcross's sincerity is not in question, but there is something remarkably superficial in pitting the human interests of the Cambodian people against what he calls 'strategic design' – an abstract concept. The whole purpose of Nixon's policy in South-East Asia was to save the world, including the people of South-East Asia, from the advance of communism. But in addition the war thrust on him by his predecessors had left him with a heavy responsibility for the young Americans engaged in it. In a TV interview he said to David Frost, in defence of the Cambodian operations: 'My responsibility was to protect those men.' We shall come later to a most vehement attack on Nixon as a result of the incursion of the Americans into Cambodia in the following year. In the case of the 1969 bombing, there is the special charge that it was conducted in secret.

In his memoirs Nixon supplies three defences of the secrecy: (1) Prince Sihanouk, head of the Cambodian government, was favourable to the bombing, but could not say so officially; (2) As long as the bombing remained secret, the North Vietnamese could hardly protest since they kept denying that they had any troops in Cambodia; (3) Nixon wanted to provoke as little public outcry as possible at the outset of his presidency. He compared his action, in replying to Frost, to Eisenhower's on the eve of Normandy. Once again, the ambiguity of the American position presents itself. Half a million of their troops were engaged in Vietnam, but were they technically at war? Nixon's secrecy on this occasion was the kind of exercise which could seldom be justified in peacetime and in war only, perhaps, if successful.

With or without the bombing of Cambodia, Nixon's efforts to bring peace in Vietnam, in spite of endless exertions by Kissinger, made no headway in 1969. In March he had confidently told the Cabinet that the war would be over in a year. He and Kissinger took all sorts of initiatives with that intention, but the North Vietnamese were all too well aware of the growing hostility to the war in America, even though the majority still favoured a strong line. The North Vietnamese could calculate that the opposition in America would steadily escalate. There was no reason why they should fit in with American designs. From August 1969 Kissinger took part in a series of cloak-and-dagger meetings with the North Vietnamese which by and large proved futile. The bombing in the end helped to bring about a more or less honorable solution. There is no sign that the negotiations in themselves led anywhere.

Nixon tried desperately to establish a relationship with Ho Chi Minh. On 25 August Ho sent him a cold rebuff but Ho himself died soon afterwards. His death, whatever its long-term implications, did not affect the immediate conflict. Nixon could not let matters drift indefinitely. He fixed on 1 November as a kind of ultimatum deadline. He indicated that there must be some response by then from North Vietnam – or else. But as the date drew near, the cards in his hand were not getting stronger. His ultimatum only had a chance of succeeding if he could convince the communists that he could 'depend on solid support at home', if they decided to call his bluff. But the chance that he would in fact be able to display such support was becoming increasingly slim. The protests became more and more widespread and violent. On 15 October a quarter of a million people descended on Washington in a so-called moratorium, a central feature of a nation-wide protest. A leading writer on the *Washington Post*, no friend at any time of Nixon, wrote on 7 October: 'It is becoming more obvious with every passing day that the men and the movement that broke Lyndon Johnson's authority in 1968 are out to break Richard Nixon in 1969. The likelihood is great that they will succeed again.'

The North Vietnamese left him in no doubt that they were aware of his domestic dilemma. His 1 November ultimatum seemed to have failed in advance. He now began to pursue a policy of increased Vietnamization, a building-up of the power of the South Vietnamese to defend themselves. This made good sense on paper, but there were not likely to be any immediate dividends. When Kissinger brought Dobrynin, the Soviet Ambassador, to see him on 20 October, he was in no mood to reveal any weakness. He never lost sight of the ultimate objective of his Russian policy, which was one of peace through strength, but also through communication.

Dobrynin began to inform him that Moscow was not satisfied with the present state of relations between the USSR and the USA. 'Moscow', he informed Nixon, 'feels that the President should be frankly told that the method of solving the Vietnam question through the use of military force is not only without perspective, but also extremely dangerous.' He agreed that if the United States were tempted to make profit from Soviet-Chinese relations at the Soviet Union's expense, they would be in for unpleasant surprises. Nixon was having none of that. What he said about China is worth recording: 'Anything we have done or are doing with respect to China is in no sense designed to embarrass the Soviet Union. On the contrary, China and the United States cannot tolerate having a situation develop in which we are enemies, any more than we want to be permanent enemies of the Soviet Union. Therefore we expect to make moves in trade and exchanges of persons and eventually in diplomacy. I want to repeat that this is not directed against the Soviet Union.'

As regards Vietnam, he warned the Russian Ambassador that if the Soviet Union found it possible to do something real in Vietnam and the Vietnam War ended, *then* something dramatic might be done to improve the USA–Soviet relationship. Then, but not till then. Kissinger's opinion of the way Nixon handled the matter is worth recording: 'I wager', he said, 'that no one has ever talked to him that way in his entire career. It was extraordinary. No President has ever laid it on the line to them like that.' But Kissinger was everlastingly a flatterer, especially in dealing with Nixon.

The great question was what posture Nixon would assume in his televized address to the nation of 3 November. There was a strong recommendation from most of his advisers that he should re-emphasize his desire for peace. Kissinger alone, it seems, favoured a hard line. Mansfield, the powerful leader of the Democratic majority in the Senate, offered Nixon a chance to 'get off the hook' in Vietnam; to blame the war on his Democratic predecessors and clear out as fast as possible. Nixon, rejecting this soft option, was acting entirely in accordance with his idea of principle.

On the whole, Nixon refrains from boasting about the consequences of his speeches, though he likes recalling them, but he claims a lot for his effort on 3 November. 'Very few speeches', he writes, 'actually influence the course of history. The speech of 3 November was one of them.' He was prepared for plenty of hostile reactions, but it was a great surprise to him that the response was, on balance, overwhelmingly favourable. 'To you,' he had called, 'the great silent majority of my fellow Americans, I ask for your support.' And that is exactly what they gave him. For the first time the great silent majority made itself heard. Messages of support poured in from every side.

Always, however, his eyes were set on the world picture – the world beyond Vietnam. In August he had won the narrowest of majorities in the Senate, 50-50 with the Chairman giving him the casting vote, in favour of America manufacturing the missile ABM. He is convinced, rightly it still seems, that without that demonstration of support for a powerful American defence system, he would never have reached an agreement with the Russians over arms limitation. But the Vietnamese question would not let him alone for long. His public opinion rating rose to 68 per cent – the highest since his inauguration – but he was well aware that he could not sustain that degree of confidence unless he soon produced some initiative and some results to show for it.

His dealings with Congress were bound to be awkward. He was the first President to take office for 120 years with both Houses of Congress against him. On defence matters he could usually rely on some sort of majority, though a tiny one over the ABM. But in 1969, he sent over forty *domestic* proposals to Congress affecting tax reform, foreign aid, electoral reform, population growth, crime and drug and pornography control. Only two of these proposals were passed. There is no need to be particularly sympathetic to the conservative trend expressed in some of these, but they represented a bold and coherent approach, though one which was bound to run into trouble with the Democratic majority.

There were not a few exhilarating moments, notably the landing on the moon. Nixon watched Neil Armstrong step on to the moon, heard his voice come through loud and clear and then spoke from the heart: 'Because of what you have done, the heavens have become part of man's world. And as you talk to us from the Sea of Tranquility, it inspires us to redouble our efforts to bring peace and tranquility to earth.'

Less pleasantly, it was found necessary to revert to wire-tapping. Edgar Hoover, head of the FBI, told Nixon that tapping was the only really effective means of uncovering 'leakers'. Tapping had been authorized by every President starting with Roosevelt. Johnson had been driven almost frantic by leaks, and by April Nixon and Kissinger felt their foreign policy seriously imperilled. Nixon informs us that he wanted maximum secrecy on the wire-tap project but also instructed that the tape be taken off as soon as possible. The average number of warrantless wire-taps per year was less than in any administration since Roosevelt's. And it was not till 1972 that the Supreme Court ruled that national security taps on American citizens must be authorized by a court order warrant if the subject had no 'significant connection with a foreign power, its agents or agencies'. By that time the last of his national security taps had been removed.

Bill Safire, very close to Nixon, makes bitter fun of Kissinger for his subsequent attempts to dissociate himself from the wire-tapping policy. Safire will not accept his claims in this respect, all the more because he himself was tapped on Kissinger's instructions. How far the policy was Nixon's and how far Kissinger's will never be fully elucidated. Nixon, in retrospect, does not appear too happy about it, but declares with some justice that without secrecy 'there would have been no opening to China, no SALT agreement with the Soviet Union and no peace agreement ending the Vietnam war'. It is certain that the leakers imperilled secrecy. It is also admitted that the tappers failed to catch them.

Nixon felt at the end of 1969 that his administration was settling down. Admittedly the friction between Rogers and Kissinger was getting worse all the time. Nixon cannot be exonerated here. He tells us himself that with the 'plan to direct foreign policy from the White House, whoever was his National Security Adviser was bound to be closer to him on the biggest questions, making the position of the Secretary of State increasingly intolerable'. Kissinger's ambitions were remorseless. What might have survived on a basis of live-and-let-live become more and more unworkable.

A heavy task fell on Haldeman who, in Nixon's words, had to 'hold the whole thing together' and 'make the wheels go round'. John Ehrlichman had been gradually moved into the position of co-ordinating all domestic programmes and issues. In the next few months Chuck Colson was to join the inner circle as counsel to the President.

Haldeman was Nixon's Chief of Staff and, over a long period, the most important single individual serving him. He was a Christian Scientist, a teetotaller, a fanatical Nixon man since 1956. He was the former head of the J. Walter Thompson advertising agency in Los Angeles, a super organizer in intention. 'He does not want to organize,' said Haldeman, of his revered President. 'He wants to *be* organized.' He quotes in his memoirs, apparently with pride, a profile of himself in the White House:

Harry Robbins Haldeman is, as he once put it, Richard Nixon's son-of-a-bitch. He sits one hundred gold-carpeted feet down the hall from the Oval Office, glowering out at the world from under a crew cut that would flatter a drill instructor, with a gaze that would freeze Medusa. He is neither quite so forbidding as he looks, nor quite so fierce as his reputation as the keystone of a Berlin Wall around Mr Nixon; he even has a sense of humor, about subjects other than his boss. But he is the man who says *no* for the President of the United States, a mission he executes with a singleness of purpose and an authority that are respected – and feared – throughout official Washington. . . .

Haldeman's loyalty to Nixon was wholly admirable. Possibly, if it had not been so complete, he would have restrained his master somewhat more effectively. But one must refrain from dragging in British analogies and sighing for the secretary of a British Cabinet, who would be better placed to say to a Prime Minister contemplating an indiscretion, 'PM, you know you cannot do that.'

John Ehrlichman is a slightly more elusive figure, if only because, unlike Haldeman and Colson, he has not yet written his memoirs. His two novels based on his White House experiences are brilliant, cynical reconstructions. He is referred to as an idealist, with his own vision of a better America. Possibly for that reason he seems to have been more embittered by his eventual fall than any of the others. Like Haldeman, he was from California and a Christian Scientist (there were several more Christian Scientists in the entourage). He and Haldeman were referred to frequently as 'the Germans'. In the end, the combination of these two men was helpful to neither.

Gerald Ford is very severe on them: 'Haldeman, Ehrlichman and a few of their associates on the White House staff viewed Congress in much the same way that the chairman of the board of a large corporation regards his regional sales managers. We existed, they seemed to believe, as if we were a coequal branch of government. And this from former advance men whose only political experience had been to hold Nixon's raincoat and organize his crowds.'

I have not at the time of writing met Bob Haldeman, though the firm of which I am chairman was happy to publish his book of memoirs, nor have I met John Ehrlichman. But I have met Chuck Colson several times, had prolonged talks with him and listened to him orating movingly on Christian issues. He was often referred to as 'the hatchet man' who had said he would walk over his own grandmother to serve the President and who, in his own frank admission, was responsible for many a dirty trick, which he now regrets bitterly. Even before he went to prison, after the disclosures connected with Watergate, he had undergone a very remarkable Christian conversion. When he emerged, he not only wrote a deeply impressive Christian apologia, *Born Again*, but initiated a nationwide Christian Prison Fellowship. Some of us in Britain have paid him the sincere compliment of setting up a fellowship on similar lines in Britain and have drawn the utmost encouragement from his inspiration and practical assistance. Haldeman and others have made him something of a scapegoat and accused him in their various writings of bringing out the worst in Nixon. In so far as he did so, he was certainly not acting in isolation. No penitent has ever drawn strength more promptly from his own downfall, to come to the rescue of others.

5
The War Comes Home
1970

Nixon began 1970 with a large if precarious majority of public opinion behind him, but with a very critical Congress and dissident protest growing ever more violent. On the home front there was much progress of various kinds. Nixon, while never a radical on school desegregation and other issues of civil rights, carried on the forward movement. He is entitled to quote Pat Moynihan, admittedly a minister involved, but a notably independent Democrat. Moynihan wrote at the beginning of 1970: 'There has been more change in the structure of American public-school education in the past month than in the past hundred years.'

But the poisoned legacy of the Vietnam War tainted all it came near to at home and abroad. David Frost, in the book arising out of his interviews with Nixon, sharply condemns some of the steps which Nixon took in the light of the war situation, but he does not underestimate the effect of the war on Nixon's attitudes or in bringing about his downfall. He wrote:

The Vietnam war was a catalyst. There could be no greater mistake on anyone's part than to define it as limited. The war *was* limited from the standpoint of military commitment and national objectives. But those very constraints turned it into an unlimited internal political struggle from which no theatre of national life was remote.... Nixon was not really all that paranoiac. He was in a sense right.... The demonstrators were certainly fighting against his war. [But in his fairer moments David Frost never claimed that this was 'Nixon's war'.] . . . And as long as that war required, as it did, a pervasive political commitment on the part of the American people, they were undermining that commitment. They were not only prolonging the war; they were losing it. They were the enemy.

Except for the reference to 'his war', Nixon could not have put it better. In his memoirs he makes the further point that now the passions of 1970, for example, have cooled down, it is hard to realize the desperate state of affairs that was developing at that time. The whole fabric of American order was threatened. Be that as it may, intelligence sources indicated early in 1970 that the North Vietnamese had begun moving large numbers of troops and equipment into Cambodia and Laos, and that communist infiltration from North into South Vietnam was continuously expanding. On 21 February, Kissinger had his second secret meeting in Paris with the North Vietnamese. He came back very optimistic. At a further meeting on 16 March, Kissinger told the North Vietnamese that if a settlement could be reached all the American troops could be out of Vietnam within sixteen months. They 'appeared interested but remained non-committal.' Well they might; they could safely reckon that things were going their way.

On 18 March, while visiting Moscow, the Cambodian Head of State, Prince Sihanouk, was overthrown by a bloodless military *coup* that brought to power General Lon Nol. Sihanouk had managed to preserve a clever neutrality. Lon Nol was a strong anti-communist. It must be emphasized that Lon Nol's *coup* came as a complete surprise not only to Nixon but also to the CIA. 'What the hell do those clowns do out there in Langley?' demanded the President impatiently.

By the end of April, the communists had a quarter of Cambodia under control and were closing in on the capital. It seemed clear that Lon Nol needed help to survive. The communist sanctuaries, as they were called, were in two main areas. Nixon became convinced that the most effective help that could be given Lon Nol would be to invade the sanctuaries with American troops and South Vietnamese. He tells us that he never had any illusions about the shattering effect the decision to go into Cambodia would have on public opinion at home. 'I knew that opinions among my major foreign policy advisers were deeply divided over the issue of widening the war. I recognized that it could mean personal and political catastrophe for me and my administration.' There could be nothing ignoble about a decision to go ahead under these circumstances, though it might or might not be wise.

When he spoke to the American people the uproar was already tremendous. He stressed that this was not 'an invasion of Cambodia'. The sanctuaries were completely occupied and controlled by North Vietnamese forces. 'We could withdraw once they had been driven out and once their military supplies were destroyed.' The purpose was not to expand the war into Cambodia but to end the war in Vietnam by making peace possible. The United States of America could not act like 'a pitiful helpless giant'; otherwise the forces of totalitarianism and anarchy would threaten free nations and free institutions throughout the world.

The night before he made the speech, he had been unable to sleep. In his own eyes, this was probably the hardest decision that he ever took. He still insists, as in his talks with David Frost, that in a military sense the operation was a complete success. It was one of the three most successful military operations of the war. By the end of June the sanctuaries had been eliminated and the American and South Vietnamese troops were withdrawn. In the long run the incursion did him so much harm with American public opinion that any military advantage was more than outweighed.

The tone of moral condemnation adopted by Shawcross, however, seems to me not only unjustified but at times hysterical. The Shawcross thesis, simply stated, is that it was the Nixon–Kissinger invasion of Cambodia which ultimately led to the country being taken over by the communists. He accepts that the later mass murders called – not unfairly – genocide were the acts of the communist Khmer Rouge, but insists that, indirectly, Nixon and Kissinger were responsible. An English friend of mine who was in an official position in Cambodia in exactly those years treats the Shawcross thesis as too fantastic to take seriously, bearing no relation to anything happening on the ground.

69

For the moment I must leave the last word with Kissinger. Shawcross had the opportunity of reading Nixon's memoirs, Kissinger of reading Shawcross.

Without our incursion, the communists would have taken over Cambodia years earlier. The bizarre argument has indeed been made, with a glaring lack of substantiation, that the cruelty of the Khmer Rouge in victory was the product of five years of American and Cambodian efforts to resist them. No one can accept this as an adequate explanation except apologists for the murderous Khmer Rouge. Sihanouk does not believe this; they were men he had kicked out of Cambodia in 1967 because they were a menace to his country. He told me in April 1979 that the Khmer Rouge leaders were 'always killers' from the beginning.

Nevertheless he admits that, in view of the effect on public opinion, 'whether to attack the sanctuaries was a close call on which honest and serious individuals might well differ'. The ultimate destruction of Cambodia could not have happened if American support had continued to be forthcoming. But the murderers, the authors of the genocide, were not Americans or products of American policy.

Wave after wave of violent campus unrest had marked the spring of 1970. In particular bombings were increasing and radical groups, in Nixon's phrase, 'openly encouraged the bombing of institutions of which they disapproved'. Nixon about this time used an expression which proved unfortunate. 'I have seen them,' he said about the American troops in Vietnam. 'They are the greatest. You see these bums blowing up the campuses. . . .' The word soon got round that he called all students 'bums'.

On 4 May the dreadful news came through that, at a demonstration at Kent State University, the National Guard had opened fire and four students had been shot dead. Nixon felt utterly dejected when he read that the father of one of the dead girls had told a reporter 'my child was not a bum'. A nationwide wave of campus protests followed. A national day of protest was called and took place in Washington on 9 May.

On the night of 8 May Nixon slept for a few hours and then went to the Lincoln sitting-room. He put on a record of Rachmaninoff's Second Piano Concerto and sat listening to the music. Manolo, his devoted manservant, came in to ask him if he would like some tea or coffee. He could see through the window small groups of young people gathering between the White House and the Washington monument. Nixon said to Manolo that the Lincoln Memorial at night was the most beautiful sight in Washington; Manolo said that he had never seen it. The President said to him impulsively, 'Let us go look at it now.' There followed his famous walkabout among the students. He dictated a long memorandum immediately afterwards; it occupies half a dozen pages in his memoirs. A few extracts are given below.

'I walked over to a group of them and shook hands,' he writes. 'They were not unfriendly. They seemed somewhat overawed and of course quite surprised.... I said "I know that probably most of you think I am an SOB but I want you to know that I understand just how you feel."' He recalled that at the time of Munich he thought that Chamberlain was the greatest man alive and Churchill was a madman. In retrospect he realized he was wrong. Chamberlain was a good man but Churchill was a wiser one. And so the discussion continued with the group growing from eight or ten to thirty. One of the students spoke up and said, 'I hope you realize that we are willing to die for what we believe in.' Nixon replied, 'I certainly realize that. Do you realize that many of us when we were your age were also willing to die for what we believed in and are willing to do so today?' He touched on a number of other themes, including the spiritual hunger 'which all of us have and which of course has been the great mystery of life from the beginning of time'. Other accounts have been given of this extraordinary night-time session which seek to trivialize his style of trying to communicate with the students. But taking his account as substantially correct, as we must, we can surely find something gallant and certainly nothing ludicrous in the whole adventure.

A few words must be said here about what was called the Huston plan, though nothing was known about it publicly in 1970. Later, at the time of the Watergate outcry and move towards impeachment, it was published by John Dean, the President's defecting special counsel. The background of the plan was the ever greater activity of political terrorists urging murder and bombing. Nixon writes fairly enough today: 'Now that this season of mindless terror has fortunately passed, it is difficult, perhaps impossible, to convey a sense of the pressures that were influencing my actions and reactions during this period.' He goes on to refer to 'this epidemic of unprecedented domestic terrorism' that forced him to find unusual countervailing measures.

No one could question the need to co-ordinate the activities of the various intelligence agencies. In 1970 Hoover, under some provocation, had cut off all liaison between the FBI and the CIA. A strong committee was set up. Tom Huston, a young lawyer and former Defence Intelligence Agency aide, was made responsible for drawing up a plan. Various methods were suggested which might euphemistically be described as doubtfully legal. Nixon nevertheless approved the plan, but Hoover objected. Then, five days before the plan could be implemented, Nixon withdrew his approval. 'The irony of the controversy', he writes, 'did not become apparent until a 1975 investigation revealed that the investigative techniques which would have been involved had not only been carried out long before I approved the plan, but continued to be carried out after I had rescinded my approval of it.' But that was not something that the American public wanted to hear, and when Nixon was being impeached they had not heard of it. He is entitled to quote the words of Senator Frank Church (Chairman of the Committee on Inter-Agency Intelligence) in hearings on intelligence agency activities: 'The Huston plan was limited to techniques far more restrictive than the far-reaching methods that were employed by the FBI during the years that we have reviewed.' But at the time of Watergate, Senator Frank Church had not yet made that pronouncement.

In the Middle East, the new emphasis of the Nixon–Kissinger policy became visible in connection with the affairs of Jordan. Nixon was convinced that it was in America's interests to halt the Soviet domination of the Arab Middle East. To do so would require a broadening of American relations with the Arab countries. America's Middle Eastern policy under Presidents Kennedy and Johnson was aimed primarily at supplying the arms and money to enable Israel to defend itself against its potential enemies. But Nixon had much more complicated and far-reaching aims in view.

Many members of the American Jewish community had decided to boycott the State visit in 1970 of President Pompidou of France as a protest against his recent sale to Libya of more than a hundred jet-fighters. Neither Governor Rockefeller nor Mayor Lindsay would officially receive him in New York. Nixon regarded this as intolerable humbug or political cowardice. He flew to New York and attended the public dinner that Rockefeller and Lindsay were boycotting.

Nixon went further. In March 1970 he decided to postpone the delivery of Phantom jets to Israel. Israel was already in a strong military position. He could slow down the arms race without disturbing the military balance in the region; he believed that American influence in the Middle East depended on their renewing diplomatic relationships with Egypt and Syria. Not surprisingly he received strong protests from Mrs Meir, Prime Minister of Israel, and from many of Israel's supporters in Congress. During the months that followed, Nixon insisted that he had no illusions about Soviet motives in the Middle East. As explained in a memorandum to Kissinger, he made an absolute commitment that Israel would always have 'an edge'. But they must realize that he must carry with him the whole of American public opinion and not be dominated by the Jewish vote.

He told President Pompidou that he was trying to construct a completely new set of power relationships in the Middle East, not only between Israel and the Arabs, but also among the United States, Western Europe and the Soviet Union. In September 1970 this new and rather delicate policy was put to the test of war. The Palestinian extremist guerillas, backed by Syrian arms and aid, had stirred up the Palestinian refugees living in Jordan and threatened to provoke a civil war against the régime of King Hussein. Kissinger advised Nixon that the Soviets were at the bottom of the aggression. Mrs Meir, in the United States on an unofficial visit, called on him in a very stern mood. She insisted that the President should go to the Soviets directly and demand an adjustment of the situation. Shortly afterwards, the news reached the White House that Syrian tanks had crossed the Jordanian border. Nixon decided to pursue 'a very hard but quiet line. I authorized Kissinger to call Ambassador Rabin of Israel and suggest that he inform his government that we would be fully in support of Israeli air strikes on Syrian forces in Jordan *if* this became necessary to avoid a Jordanian defeat. I decided to put 20,000 American troops on alert and moved additional naval forces into the Mediterranean.' In the end, Jordan saved itself. The Israeli Ambassador seemed well pleased with the Nixon–Kissinger exercise. He ascribed Hussein's victory to the tough American position, the Israeli threat and the superb fighting by Hussein's troops. The new policy of balance had paid off this time.

In the autumn there were somewhat critical situations to be dealt with in Cuba and Chile. The first passed off without the public being aware that a Cuban crisis resembling that of 1962 had loomed up. There was no doubt that at one point the Soviets were constructing a submarine base on the shores of Alcatraz Island off Cuba's southern coast. But Nixon and Kissinger obtained an assurance that they were not doing anything in Cuba that would contradict the understanding of 1962. The submarine base was discontinued accordingly.

Nixon has been much attacked over his interference in Chile. In September 1970 a pro-Castro Marxist, Salvador Allende, came in first with a 36.3 plurality. He still required to be chosen President. Presidents Kennedy and Johnson had authorized CIA expenditure in past years to avert a communist take-over in Chile. Nixon, well aware that the communists themselves were supplying external funds to help Allende, carried on the Kennedy–Johnson tradition and authorized the CIA to support his opponents. But this policy proved quite ineffective. Nixon told the CIA to drop it. Allende was inaugurated President of Chile on 3 November without intervention by Nixon.

Nixon does not mention in his memoirs a line he took in 1970 which appeals particularly to myself and the many who think like me in all countries. The report of the American Commission on Obscenity and Pornography produced a total conflict between the majority and the minority. The majority finding in favour of a far-reaching removal of controls was overwhelmingly rejected by a 60–5 roll-call of the Senate in contemptuous terms. Here was an issue where for once the Senate and the President were in total agreement. 'I have evaluated that report', he said, 'and categorically reject its morally bankrupt conclusions and majority recommendation.... The Commission on Pornography and Obscenity has performed a disservice and I totally reject its report.' In the following year I myself initiated a British inquiry into pornography. We were indeed grateful for the conclusions reached by the President of the United States and the Senate.

Now the 1970 congressional campaign was getting under way, but Nixon had decided not to do any active campaigning himself. He thought that in the Vice-President, Spiro Agnew, there was 'the perfect spokesman to reach the silent majority on the social issue'. Two gifted Democratic writers had floated the idea that the average American voter in the next election was a forty-seven-year-old housewife from the outskirts of Dayton, Ohio. They were setting out to persuade Democrats to stop playing to what Nixon called 'the fashionable but unrepresentative constituencies of the young, the poor, the racial minorities'. Whether at the time this was or was not clever politics hardly concerns us now.

As remarked before, Nixon was a strong conservative whose ideas would not at all points appeal to the present author. He believed with all his heart that in the long run his conservative social and economic policies would be best for everyone, including the weak and the outcasts.

In the result, the Republicans lost nine seats in the House of Representatives and gained two in the Senate, after very strenuous electioneering by Nixon in the later stages, in the teeth of some unpleasant opposition. He describes this as an excellent showing, though he admits that the TV networks and the news magazines, by now congenitally hostile to him, treated the election as a significant political failure.

He formed a resolution at this time that he would 'firmly and flatly' keep out of the re-election campaign until as late as possible in 1972. But Chuck Colson insists from first-hand knowledge that Nixon was always burning to play an active part in the campaign. Haldeman and Colson tried to prevent him unsuccessfully. His determination to stay out, in so far as it existed, was short-lived. Democratic Presidents since Roosevelt had revelled in exploiting the advantage that went with being the party in the White House. He intended to do at least as much.

'I told my staff', said Nixon, 'that we should come up with the kind of imaginative dirty tricks that our Democratic opponents used against us so effectively in previous campaigns.' John Mitchell would be his campaign manager and Chuck Colson would act as his political 'point man'. This was the role for which Eisenhower had cast Nixon as Vice-President. He refers to Colson's instinct for the 'political jugular', with no indication that this was an unpleasing role. He was confident that he could win the election contest on the *issues* in 1972. 'That only reinforced my determination not to let the other side be politically tougher than we were.' In the end his team would be convicted of having been not only tougher but less scrupulous than what was permitted by conventional standards. He will never admit that this was the truth. He will never be proved right or wrong.

As 1970 ended, what was to be memorable about Nixon's presidency and what was to be calamitous was still to come.

6
Two Kinds of Conscience
1971

The first few months of 1971 were what Nixon was later to call 'the lowest point' of his first term as President. It seemed possible to him at one moment that he might not even be renominated as presidential candidate. He dropped continuously in the polls while the Democrat Muskie rose steadily.

A year later (9 January 1972) he was able to record in his diary that the past year (his fifty-ninth) had been, from the standard of accomplishment, perhaps the most successful so far. The uncertainty, glorious or otherwise, of political life could hardly be better demonstrated – except by the catastrophe to come.

At the beginning of 1971, the economy was in a bad way with no sign of immediate improvement. Unemployment was the highest since 1961. The dollar was at its lowest since 1949. The prospect of a breakthrough, either with Russia or China or both, was discouraging. Victory or even an honourable settlement in Vietnam seemed as far away as ever. The hatred of the war, even though in theory a large majority of the public supported it, took a more and more violent form. The doctrine of unlawful dissent, in other words the moral right to break the law in the name of conscience, was being propounded skilfully with scant regard for ordinary scruples.

The second part of the year saw what Nixon called a series of 'stunning successes'. They certainly justified hopes of far-reaching international agreements. But in the course of the summer the unconstitutional pressures were to drive him into procedures which were to seem at least as unconstitutional and in a President even more deplorable when brought into the light of day. Chuck Colson assures me that the incursion into Laos in February of that year had lasting effects. It was an operation carried out primarily by the South Vietnamese forces with American air cover and artillery support. There was reasonable moral justification in the use being made of Laos by the North Vietnamese. Nixon describes the net result as a military success, but a psychological defeat. Colson recalls the serious disappointment at the failure of the South Vietnamese to live up to expectations and the resulting scepticism about the policy of Vietnamization. A certain desperation entered into the atmosphere of the White House.

By the late spring, progress was at last being made in the search for a new relationship with the Soviet Union and China, publicly in the first, secretly in the second case. SALT talks on disarmament had been bogged down since 1969. The Russians wanted an agreement confined to defensive systems; the Americans insisted that it should include offensive weapons. Nixon and Kissinger were not to be put off; they pegged steadily away.

Suddenly on 26 March 1971 the Russian Ambassador appeared with a suggestion which went a long way to giving the Americans what they wanted. Nixon stood firm against last-minute pressure from American 'doves' to accept the Russian proposal as it stood. He stuck to his consistent belief that you do not get anywhere with the Russians unless you negotiate from strength. Finally he appeared before the television cameras in the White House briefing-room on 20 May: 'As you know', he began, 'the Soviet-American talks on limiting nuclear arms have been deadlocked for over a year. As a result of negotiations involving the highest level of both governments, I am announcing today a significant development in breaking the deadlock.' His language was studiously vague, but within himself he felt sure that at last he and his government were 'on their way'.

June 12 was a delightful occasion – the day of Tricia's wedding to Ed Cox, a young lawyer much esteemed by her parents.

Four hundred guests attended the wedding in the rose garden of the White House. Tricia wrote about it lyrically: 'The rose garden was a crown of natural beauty, with the gazebo the most spectacular jewel of the crown. Flowers which were exquisite in their own right were intertwined with one another and out of this composition emerged a creation of beauty that surpassed the beauty of the individual flowers. For once, mankind had improved on nature.' At the reception afterwards, with the band playing 'Thank Heaven for Little Girls', Nixon danced with Tricia, then with Pat, 'an excellent dancer'. The guests broke into enthusiastic applause as she, in his words, 'steered him round the floor'. Then he danced with Julie and then with Johnson's daughter, Lynda Bird, whom he saw standing alone. Nixon remarks in his memoirs, 'Sometimes our family was called square; as far as we were concerned that was just fine.' There could never be any question about their mutual devotion. 'June 12 was a day', writes Nixon, 'that all of us will always remember, because all of us were beautifully and simply happy.' It was just as well that they could not foresee what was immediately in store for them.

On the next day, 13 June, the *New York Times* began to publish the so-called Pentagon Papers, the most serious leak of classified secret material in the history of America. James Reston, the foremost writer on the *New York Times* began by writing that they revealed the 'deceptive and stealthy American involvement in the war under Presidents Kennedy and Johnson'. On the face of it, those were the Presidents whose reputations stood to suffer. But Nixon was well aware that the real intention of the publication by the violently anti-war *New York Times* was to discredit his current policies in Vietnam. The discussions with Russia and China were at a particularly delicate stage. 'China was', as Safire points out, 'absolutely insistent on secrecy and suspicious of any tricks.' Here was the premier newspaper in the United States trumpeting top-secret documents about the Kennedy/Johnson years every day. Who knew what they would publish next? One may say in passing that it is inconceivable that government secrets could be leaked on this scale in Britain, or published in a leading British newspaper. Even in America, where the conditions were less secretive, it was an extraordinary defiance of ordinary decencies.

'Nixon', continues Safire, 'was beside himself at the Press's arrogance at deciding for itself what was secret and what was not; worried that if the Press got away with this, they would feel free to reveal any secret at all; and convinced that a supine acceptance of this stripping-away of the United States' government's ability to deal confidentially was harmful to his summit negotiations.' Nixon, like Johnson before him, was already disgusted with the endless leaks and most of all with those responsible for this new development. He was fully entitled, indeed it was his bounden duty, to react strongly and take every legal step to stop publication if possible.

But on 30 June he was defeated by the Supreme Court who refused by six votes to three to prevent publication. Efforts to prosecute the man believed to be responsible for the leak, Daniel Ellsberg, were now redoubled. Nixon considered, not unreasonably, that Ellsberg, in revealing government foreign policy secrets during wartime, had done something despicable and contemptible. On 28 June a Los Angeles grand jury indicted Ellsberg on one count of theft of government property and one count of unauthorized possession of documents and writings related to national defence. He was given a hero's welcome by admirers outside the court house. It was not only Ellsberg who was under suspicion; there was reason to suppose that a much wider conspiracy was at work. Nixon now proceeded to over-react wildly, if understandably.

To his extreme indignation, he found that J. Edgar Hoover, the head of the FBI, was 'dragging his feet' for a mixture of reasons. 'Well, then', said Nixon to himself, 'if the FBI are not going to pursue the case we shall have to do it ourselves.'

At this time Ellsberg was having great success in the media with his efforts to justify unlawful dissent which, in Nixon's view, struck at the root of all coherent government. He tells us frankly in his memoirs that he did not intend to stop there. He wanted to obtain ammunition not only against Ellsberg but against the 'anti-war critics, many of whom were the same men who under Kennedy and Johnson had led us into the Vietnam morass in the first place'. To do so he went to the limit of legality – some will say beyond. On 17 July 1971 Ehrlichman assigned Egil 'Bud' Krogh, a young lawyer on the Domestic Council staff, to 'head the leak project'. David Young, a lawyer who was formerly a Kissinger aide, Howard Hunt, a former CIA agent, and G. Gordon Liddy, a former FBI man, worked with him. Their job was plugging leaks. Young jokingly put up a sign establishing himself as a plumber, a name Nixon first heard of eighteen months later. The damage done to Nixon and some of his associates when the existence of 'the plumbers' was discovered was far-reaching. Their importance became very much exaggerated. There were never four of them and they began to disband in September. But the mischief was done.

There is no evidence that Nixon authorized them to undertake any illegal action, though he admits motivating Krogh in what he calls 'the strongest terms'. But they soon went ahead in reckless fashion. On Labour Day weekend, the 'plumbers' organized a break-in at the office of Ellsberg's psychiatrist in an attempt to get information from his files on Ellsberg's motivation, his further intentions and any possible co-conspirators. The object in black and white terms was to discredit him, and more significantly to defeat the movement which he was inspiring all too successfully. Already on 20 May, as mentioned above, Nixon had announced what seemed a fundamental breakthrough in American–Soviet relations.

Nixon still believes that he was not told about the break-in at the time. Colson is quite certain that Nixon was not told in advance; only he himself or John Ehrlichman could have told him and neither did so. The following sentence, however, cannot be ignored in his memoirs: 'Given the tempo of those tense and bitter times and the peril I perceived, I cannot say that had I been informed of it beforehand. I would have automatically considered it unprecedented, unwarranted or unthinkable.' But there is no doubt that it was illegal and Nixon seems to be telling us that he would not necessarily have ruled out illegal action during those moments of crisis. There was nothing necessarily illegal about establishing the 'plumbers', but if *he* authorized the Ellsberg break-in, which he is confident he did not, he would have crossed the borderline and with his eyes open flouted the law.

Today his attitude seems to border on inconsistency. On

the one hand he admits that he was 'sometimes drawn into the very frame of mind that I so despised in the "anti-war movement". They came to justify any action that appealed to them as likely to force an immediate end to the war. I was similarly driven to preserve the government's ability and to conduct it in the way that I felt would best bring peace.' In other words, no holds barred on either side. What is a little puzzling is that, while he regrets being driven into an attitude similar to theirs, he still insists that 'in the same circumstances I would act now as I did then'.

His defence must, in the last resort, depend on the adage relied on throughout the ages by many governments, some good, some bad, in times of extreme crisis: '*Salus populi, suprema lex*'. At the time of writing it has come to light that in 1940 and 1941 the British Intelligence Services, acting no doubt on high authority, adopted every kind of method, including forgery, in total defiance of American law to discredit Americans who were trying to prevent America from being drawn into hostilities. These American citizens must be presumed to have been innocent of the kind of lawlessness indulged in by Ellsberg. 'History', says Nixon fairly enough, 'will make the final judgment on the actions, reactions and excesses of both sides; it is a judgment I do not fear.' It is at least certain that when, in a better world than this, all the books are open, there will be revealed many irregularities carried on by governments in warlike times which will shock us far more than the break-in at the psychiatrist's office.

July and August brought Nixon at last some striking encouragement. International developments began to seem to be taking shape in a pattern of his devising. On 15 July he took the whole world by surprise by announcing that he would be going to Peking. In a talk of no more than three and a half minutes he stated,

I have requested this television time to announce a major development in our efforts to build a lasting peace in the world.
Premier Chou En-lai and Dr Henry Kissinger, President Nixon's Assistant for National Security Affairs, held talks in Peking from 9 to 11 July 1971. Knowing of President Nixon's expressed desire to visit the People's Republic of China, Premier Chou En-lai, on behalf of the government of the People's Republic

of China, has extended an invitation to President Nixon to visit China at an appropriate date before May 1972. President Nixon has accepted the invitation with pleasure.

The meeting between the leaders of China and the United States is to seek the normalization of relations between the two countries and also to exchange views on questions of concern to the two sides.

The reception was thoroughly cordial in America and throughout the world, except for a few left-wing enemies at home and some extreme rightists, who regarded the visit to China as supping with the devil. In Taiwan, sadly but predictably, the reaction was one of horror.

We must retrace our steps to appreciate the background. Nixon has pointed to the beginnings of his whole China policy in an article in *Foreign Affairs* in 1967, already quoted. He said there, 'We seek an open world, a world in which no people great or small will live in angry isolation.' By the time he became President the rift between Russia and China was patent. He himself considers that the history of the relations between these two countries has been the story of a long struggle for control in the heart of Asia. More recently they have come to vie for leadership in the communist world. As soon as he took office he issued an instruction that the whole policy towards China must be reconsidered.

The first serious public step was taken in February 1970, when he sent the first foreign policy report to Congress:

The Chinese are a great and vital people who should not remain isolated from the international community. . . . The principles underlying our relations with Communist China are similar to those governing our policies toward the USSR. United States policy is not likely soon to have much impact on China's behavior, let alone its ideological outlook. But it is certainly in our interest, and in the interest of peace and stability in Asia, and the world, that we take what steps we can toward improved practical relations with Peking.

'The leaders in Peking', says Nixon, 'clearly understood the significance of the language in this report.' Events moved forward unobtrusively. Early in October 1970 Nixon gave an interview to *Time* magazine in which he said, 'If there is anything that I want to do before I die, it is to go to China. If

83

I do not, I want my children to.' Soon afterwards President Yahya Khan of Pakistan came to see him and agreed to help as an intermediary. President Ceausescu of Romania was also pressed into service. On 18 December Mao Tse-tung told his old friend, the American writer Edgar Snow, that he would be happy to talk to the President whether he came as a tourist or as a President. Obstacles obtruded themselves in various ways, but the forward movement went on.

On 6 April 1971 word was received from the American embassy in Tokyo that an American table-tennis team competing in the World Championships in Japan had been invited to visit the People's Republic of China. Messages and signals had been going backward and forward for more than two years. In the late spring of 1971 Nixon and Kissinger decided that the time had come for a major proposal. Word was conveyed to Chou En-lai that Nixon was prepared to accept 'Chou's invitation to visit Peking [which had been received early in 1971]'. Nixon proposed that Kissinger undertake a secret visit in advance in order to arrange an agenda and begin a preliminary exchange of views.

On 2 June Nixon was working in the Lincoln sitting-room after dinner when Kissinger walked in out of breath with exertion or excitement. He stood 'beaming' as Nixon read two sheets of typewritten paper. The message ran:

Premier Chou En-lai has seriously studied President Nixon's messages of 29 April, 17 May and 22 May 1971, and has reported with much pleasure to Chairman Mao Tse-tung that President Nixon is prepared to accept his suggestion to visit Peking for direct conversations with the leaders of the People's Republic of China. Chairman Mao Tse-tung has indicated that he welcomes President Nixon's visit and looks forward to that occasion when he may have direct conversations with His Excellency the President, in which each side would be free to raise the principal issue of concern to it...

Premier Chou En-lai welcomes Dr Kissinger to China as the US representative who will come in advance for a preliminary secret meeting with high level Chinese officials to prepare and make necessary arrangements for President Nixon's visit to Peking.

'This,' said Kissinger dramatically, 'this is the most important communication which has come to an American President since the end of World War II.' Nixon persuaded Kissinger to have, unusually, a glass of brandy after dinner and proposed an emotional toast to 'generations to come who might have a better chance to live in peace because of what we have done'. On the biggest issues and in times such as these their unity was complete. Kissinger made his secret journey, acted with his usual expedition, produced a brilliant summing-up after the trip and paved the way for Nixon's epoch-making announcement of 15 July.

Harold Wilson is one who has often expressed his regard for Nixon's statesmanship. Meeting Colson at a dinner in 1979, he commented, with special reference to his China break-through, 'Nixon was a Tory who was able to do Liberal things; I was a Liberal who could do Tory things.'

There were fears, genuine or otherwise, that the new under-standing with China would damage the hope of a détente with Russia. This in no way occurred. Talks facilitating better arrangements in Berlin reached a successful conclusion in late August. On 12 October a joint announcement issued in Wash-ington and Moscow confirmed that Nixon would visit the Soviet Union three months after returning from China. The USA/Soviet summit was at last possible because of two achievements. In the first place was the progress in the SALT talks which Nixon announced in May *before* the visit to Peking was made public. Second, there was progress on a Berlin settlement *after* the China announcement. Nixon is entitled to claim that his systematic pursuit of a policy of 'linkage' had paid off handsomely. Now he was going to have a China trip and a Soviet summit as well. The announcement of the Chinese visit had not retarded the Soviet summit but had accelerated it and made it more certain.

'I have always', writes Nixon, 'believed that America's economy operates best with the least possible governmental interference.' Yet he acknowledges half-ruefully that in August 1971 he proposed a series of economic controls and reforms that left even long-time wage- and price-control advocates breathless. It is indeed an ironic tale. The economy, as already mentioned, was sluggish, but along with heavy unemployment went heavy inflation in the early months of 1971. On 26 June that year he met with his economic advisers at Camp David. By this time many critics and economists were demanding some programme of mandatory control of prices and wages. Nixon, after listening to much conflicting advice and weighing the views of the experts at Camp David, declined to alter course dramatically. He designated instead an economic spokesman who would be the authoritative source for the administration's economic policy. He nominated the Secretary of the Treasury, John Connally, for this role, and the Secretary emerged with the most negative programme conceivable which came to be known as the 'Four Noes'. There would be no wage and price review board, no mandatory wage and price controls, no tax cut and no increase in government spending.

But the Connally programme, however forcibly presented by its author, had little chance of success. Discontent mounted alarmingly, in spite of a great deal of public satisfaction over the China initiative. By 6 August Connally had prepared a new and startling report at Nixon's invitation. Nixon expected something bold from Connally, but even so was taken aback by his new proposals. Connally urged in effect total war on all economic fronts, including 'across the board' wage and price control. 'I'm not sure', he said, 'that this programme will work. But I *am* sure that anything less will not work.' He advised Nixon to let the issue 'sit and simmer' for a while, until its necessity became obvious to the public.

The idea of letting the new policy 'sit and simmer' lasted no longer than the 'Four Resounding Noes' policy. In the second week of August, the British Ambassador came to the Treasury Department to ask that $3 billion should be converted into gold. Here was potentially a real monetary crisis. Nixon's response was to call a high-level meeting at Camp David on 13 August for all the best economic experts available to him. Connally described succinctly a number of drastic remedies worked out by experts. The most striking were: (1) Closing the gold window, i.e. suspending the convertibility of the dollar into gold, and (2) a ninety-day freeze on wages and prices. The second was generally accepted, but there was considerable opposition to suspending convertibility, especially from Arthur Burns, Chairman of the Federal Reserve Board, to whose opinions Nixon always attached particular weight.

After a full discussion Nixon decided to accept the main Connally proposals. The public reaction to his television speech announcing them was overwhelmingly favourable. Six weeks later 53 per cent of Americans believed that his economic policies were working, against 23 per cent who thought the opposite.

Gradually, over the next two and a half years, the wage and price controls were phased out until they were finally lifted in the spring of 1974. Nixon, sometimes accused like most public men of a reluctance to admit to error, writes with surprising severity about his 'brief fling with economic controls'. The decision to impose them he still regards as politically necessary and immensely popular in the short run. 'But in the long run I believe that it was wrong.' To his dying day he will insist that private enterprise unimpeded is more efficient than government enterprise. At the time of writing his memoirs, he was fearful that American leaders would fail to appreciate this truth. But he is not saying that the whole crisis programme of 15 August 1971 was mistaken. The decision to suspend convertibility and let the dollar float is in his eyes 'the best thing that came out of the whole economic package'.

The year was not to end without another grave international situation. On 4 November Mrs Gandhi, Prime Minister of India, called on him in the Oval Office. Eight months earlier there had been a rebellion in East Pakistan against the government of President Yahya Khan. Ten million refugees had already fled from East Pakistan into India. Nixon was aware by this time that Mrs Gandhi had 'gradually become aligned with the Soviets' and was receiving substantial military and economic aid from Moscow. He learned later that even while she was talking to Nixon and assuring him that she had no intention of indulging in military aggression against Pakistan, her generals and advisers were planning to intervene in East Pakistan and were considering contingency plans for attacking West Pakistan as well. Nixon warned her of the incalculable consequences of any attack by India on Pakistan. 'It would be impossible', he said, 'to calculate precisely the steps which other great powers might take if India were to initiate hostilities.'

A month later, regardless of all assurances given to Nixon, the Indian Army attacked East Pakistan. Fighting also erupted along the border with West Pakistan, though the Indian purpose there was uncertain. Nixon agreed with Kissinger that the United States must demonstrate their displeasure with India and their support for Pakistan. Unless the United States helped Pakistan, Iran or any other country might begin to question the dependability of American support. As Kissinger put it: 'We don't really have any choice. We can't allow a friend of ours and China's [the reference to China is notable] to get screwed in conflict with a friend of Russia.' The weakness of the American position was the hopelessness of the military situation in East Pakistan.

Nixon took a firm line with the Russians, issuing a grave warning against a full-scale Indian attack on Pakistan with Russian equipment and encouragement. Soon Yahya Khan's forces in East Pakistan surrendered unconditionally. On 17 December the crisis on the western front came to an end when Pakistan accepted the Indian offer of a cease-fire there. One cannot know what would have happened without the positive steps taken by Nixon and Kissinger. But one is inclined to agree with Nixon that they did indeed save Pakistan from disintegration. Certainly the American leaders acted with much energy and ingenuity, achieving their purpose without a head-on clash with the Soviet Union.

7
The Missionary of Peace
January – June 1972

The first half of 1972 was to see the greatest of Nixon's achievements, the visit to China in February and the Moscow summit in June. The second was impaired though not cancelled out by the dragging-on of the Vietnam War, for which the Soviet Union was in no small degree responsible. But this was also, of course, election year. The considerations involved were never absent from Nixon's mind; but it is fair to say that they never dominated his policies.

In spite of the apparent success for Nixon of the year 1971, at the beginning of 1972 Edmund Muskie, the Democratic champion of the moment, was running even with him in the public opinion polls. Nixon thought at the time that Muskie had a fair chance of beating him and that Humphrey, backed by Labour, who had come so close in 1968, would also have an excellent chance.

He was the last person to shut his eyes to political realities or to ignore the chronic advantage possessed by the Democratic Party who in 1972 out-registered the Republican Party by several million votes. It seemed increasingly likely that all the candidates would be able to campaign against a war 'that I was not going to be able to win and that I would not yet be able to end'. But there was one Democratic candidate who was far more extreme than all the others in regard to Vietnam. This was George McGovern, who boldly announced, 'If I were President it would take me twenty-four hours and the stroke of a pen to terminate all military operations in South-East Asia.' He would withdraw all troops within ninety days, whether or not the prisoners-of-war were released.

Nixon had a shrewd idea that McGovern was going just a little too far; that he would be the one Democratic candidate that he himself would be sure of beating. As the primaries developed, McGovern made more and more headway at the expense of Muskie and the other competitors. He won the important Wisconsin primary on 4 April and also one in Massachusetts and Nebraska. By the end of the spring only Humphrey and Edward Kennedy, if he were to run (which seemed unlikely after the Chappaquiddick disaster), were left to stop him. 'To me', writes Nixon, 'his steady climb was as welcome to watch as it was almost unbelievable to behold.' So fanatical an opponent of the Vietnam War was much less likely to damage his policy than a more restrained critic.

The turning-point in Nixon's march to ascendancy was the January announcement that he would shortly be setting off for China. From that moment onwards, his stock as measured by the polls moved irresistibly forward.

We must now turn back to this Chinese visit announced on 15 July. Kissinger returned to China on 20 October for planning talks. The Chinese Prime Minister, Chou En-lai, had told him that the Chinese would be in real trouble if Nixon's administration were not in power. 'He shares', reported Kissinger, 'what he described as your wish – that you should preside over the two-hundredth anniversary of America's birth.' The wish of neither was to be granted, but when 1976 came round Nixon, fallen and for the time being discredited, was invited back to China as their honoured guest. The compliment reported by Kissinger bore the flavour of Chinese courtesy, but it at least suggests that by the time Nixon himself went to China the foundations of friendship existed.

Before setting off for China, Nixon invited André Malraux to the White House. Malraux had known Mao Tse-tung and Chou En-lai in China during the 1930s and had kept in touch with them off and on since that time. Nixon asked him whether, a few years earlier, he would have thought that the Chinese leaders would agree to meet with an American President. 'This meeting was inevitable,' Malraux replied. 'Even with the Vietnam War?' Nixon asked. 'Ah yes, even so. China's action over Vietnam is an imposture. There was a period when the friendship between China and Russia was cloudless, when they allowed Russian arms to pass over their territory on the way to Vietnam. China's foreign policy is a brilliant lie! The Chinese themselves do not believe in it; they believe only in China. Only China!'

At the end of the evening Nixon escorted Malraux to his car. The Frenchman turned to the President and said: 'I am not de Gaulle [his old chief], but I know what de Gaulle would say if he were here: he would say, "All men who understand what you are embarking upon salute you."'

Nixon devotes twenty pages of his memoirs to his Chinese journey – his outstanding triumph. Only a few happenings and snatches of dialogues can be reproduced here.

On arrival, the door of the aeroplane opened; Pat and Richard Nixon stepped out. Chou En-lai stood at the foot of the ramp, hatless in the cold. Even a heavy overcoat did not hide the thinness of his frail body. 'When we were about half-way down the steps', writes Nixon, 'he began to clap. I paused for a moment and then returned the gesture according to Chinese custom. I knew that Chou had been deeply insulted by Foster Dulles's refusal to shake hands with him at the Geneva Conference in 1954. When I reached the bottom step, therefore, I made a point of extending my hand as I walked towards him. When our hands met, one era ended and another began.'

Later Chou returned to this handshake. 'Today', he said, 'we shook hands. But John Foster Dulles didn't want to do that.' 'But you said you didn't want to shake hands with him,' Nixon countered. 'Not necessarily,' Chou replied. 'I would have.' 'Well, we will shake hands,' said Nixon, and once again they shook hands across the table.

Nixon in the end had more than fifteen hours of formal talks with Chou, covering a wide range of issues and ideas. He came to know him well and like him enormously. Indeed he mentions himself as liking 'all these austere and dedicated men'. Emotionally the most dramatic moment was the meeting, at his residence, with Mao, to whom everyone showed immense deference. He reached out to grasp Nixon's hand and held it for about a minute. He was soon indulging in the humorous self-deprecation associated with the Chinese. 'The Chairman's writings', said Nixon, 'have moved the nation and changed the world.' Mao replied, 'I have only been able to change a few places in the vicinity of Peking.' 'I voted for you,' said Mao to Nixon, with a broad smile. 'When the Chairman says he voted for me', replied Nixon, 'he voted for the lesser of two evils.' 'I like rightists,' responded Mao, in great good humour, in spite of his poor state of health. 'I am comparatively happy when people on the right come into power.'

He remarked that he had not been happy with some former Presidents, including Truman and Johnson. He politely suggested that during the Eisenhower years Nixon probably 'hadn't thought things out either'.

'Mr Chairman,' said Nixon, in a key statement, 'I am aware of the fact that over a period of years my position with regard to the People's Republic was one that the Chairman and the Prime Minister totally disagreed with. What brings us together is a recognition of a new situation in the world and a recognition on our part that what is important is not a nation's internal political philosophy. What is important is its policy towards the rest of the world and towards us.'

Nixon bluntly raised the whole question of Soviet aggression from the Chinese angle. The question he asked was: 'Which danger does the People's Republic of China face? Is it the danger of American aggression or of Soviet aggression? These are hard questions, but we have to discuss them.' Mao was growing tired. The time had come to take their leave. Nixon told Mao that he recognized the risks that he and the Prime Minister had taken in inviting them there. For the American leaders it was also a difficult decision. 'But having read some of your statements', said Nixon to the Chairman, 'I know that you are one who recognizes an opportunity when it comes and then seizes the hour and seizes the day.' Mao beamed when the translator came to these words from one of his poems. As they were leaving, Mao said: 'Your book *Six Crises* is not a bad book.' He walked the visitors to the door, shuffling slowly and saying that he had not been feeling well. 'But you look very good,' said Nixon. 'Appearances are deceiving,' said Mao, with a slight shrug.

In Chinese eyes Nixon and Kissinger had been subjected to the highest test and passed it with flying colours. All went well on the social side thereafter, though Mao's wife struck a somewhat jarring note at the ballet. In the middle of the performance she turned to Nixon and asked, 'Why did you not come to China before now?'

The communiqué at the end broke diplomatic ground by stating frankly the significant differences between the two sides on major issues, rather than smoothing them over. Neither on Vietnam, nor Korea, nor Japan, nor Taiwan was there anything approaching an identity of viewpoint. Chou had said frankly on Indo-China: 'We are not in a position to settle Vietnam in talks.' Nixon said that he fully understood the limitations of the talks in that respect. 'This is simply', he went on, 'an issue in which the only gainer in having the war continue is the Soviet Union.' Chou opined that the later the Americans withdrew from Vietnam the more difficult and unsatisfactory the withdrawal would be.

What then was gained from Nixon's visit? A personal friendship between leaders who themselves might not be in power very much longer; more significantly, a breakdown of the isolation in which China had wrapped herself, or been wrapped – the future benefits of this were incalculable. But in Nixon's eyes the most vitally important section of the Shanghai communiqué was that neither nation 'should seek hegemony in the Asia Pacific region and each is opposed to efforts by any other country, or group of countries to establish such hegemony'. By this provision 'it was subtly but unmistakably made clear that both the USA and China would oppose efforts by the USSR or any other major power to dominate Asia' – and, of course, the USSR was the major power in question.

How did Nixon come to establish such a warm relationship with the Chinese leaders? Various explanations are possible. I am assuming that his feelings towards them were and have remained warm and were not contrived for purely diplomatic purposes. On the Malraux interpretation of the Chinese caring only for China, he would simply appear to them as someone who could serve their purposes. Yet one cannot quite accept this as the whole truth. David Frost shrewdly suggests that Nixon found himself instinctively at home with high-level leaders whose lives had been largely ones of struggle. Certainly in his talks with Mao, Nixon did not hesitate to exploit their common background of poverty. It remains somewhat remarkable that Nixon, whose dedication to the American system of government and to the capitalist principles of self-help, should have found so much in common with leaders who rejected those principles absolutely. And, of course, in the world of religion the conflict of ideas would be glaring.

There seems to be no text-book explanation to the question posed. We shall soon find Nixon striking up a real friendship with Brezhnev, whose social, economic and religious ideas were at least as repugnant to him. (Was he or Mao the better Marxist or in any conventional sense a Marxist at all?) The truth is that Nixon had a great capacity for liking people who were ready to like him, and that when mutual interests pointed in the same direction, he would find it easy to make and enjoy friendships irrespective of nation or creed.

Nixon was no sooner home than a new unpleasantness developed. The columnist Jack Anderson began a series of articles in which he claimed to have unearthed a major administration scandal. He produced a memorandum allegedly from Dita Beard, a lobbyist for International Telephone and Telegraph Corporation. Anderson claimed that this memorandum implied that a government anti-trust settlement with ITT had been influenced by an ITT contribution towards the upcoming Republican convention. In the end the attempt to prove the existence of a scandal evaporated. Months later both Watergate special prosecutors, Archibald Cox and Leon Jaworski, investigated the ITT case and concluded that there had been no *quid pro quo* involved in the government settlement. Even those very severe critics of Nixon found nothing to complain of in his conduct. But in the spring of 1972 the Democrats exploited the ITT issue to the utmost. The White House staff became somewhat rattled. Mitchell, the Attorney-General, and the Assistant Attorney-General, Kleindienst, were quite worn out. The government lost a massive partisan public-relations battle of which the psychological consequences would rumble on.

There was also another untoward consequence of an opposite character. The White House staff had been through a bad time and survived. There was an increased disposition to suppose that they could 'get away with anything'. The chances of a Watergate were considerably enhanced.

There was no good news from the Vietnam front. For more than a year the North Vietnamese had played what Nixon called a cynical game with the peace talks in Paris. They played the game which best suited their country, in fact. On 13 January Nixon had approved the withdrawal of 70,000 more American troops from Vietnam over the next three months. By 1 May, four months away, there would be only 69,000 Americans remaining in Vietnam and they too would be getting ready to leave.

On 25 January 1972 he felt that the veil must be drawn aside and the American public taken into his confidence. He revealed that Kissinger had been holding secret meetings with the North Vietnamese since 1969. But there had been no success and it was time to try another way. The critics of war in North Vietnam and America were denouncing Nixon for not accepting possible solutions. The public should realize that such solutions had already been rejected privately by the North Vietnamese. Nixon was ready to consider almost any potential peace agreement. The only kind of plan he would not consider was one that overthrew the South Vietnamese ally, and of course there could be no possible question of failing to secure the return of the American prisoners-of-war. The Vietnamese war and the tangled negotiations attending it added enormously to the difficulties of organizing a meaningful Soviet summit.

On 30 March the North Vietnamese launched a full-scale invasion. Over the next few weeks their main army, estimated at 120,000 troops, marched across the internationally recognized neutral territory of the demilitarized zone and pushed deep into South Vietnam. Reports poured in about their endless atrocities. On 4 April the State Department publicly announced that Soviet arms were supporting the North Vietnamese invasion. The Soviet government nevertheless continued to discuss with Kissinger the coming summit. They assured him that the North Vietnamese would adopt a very responsive approach when the private talks in Paris were resumed on 24 April. The earlier suggestion was repeated that Kissinger should make a secret visit to Moscow, so that Vietnam and other agenda items could be discussed with Brezhnev before the summit. Nixon agreed with Kissinger that he should accept this invitation, although he had no intention of allowing the North Vietnamese invasion of the South to go unchecked or unpunished.

Nixon seemed indeed, unusually for him, to be erring on the side of optimism. He felt that the North Vietnamese invasion was a sign of desperation. He had decided to go all-out to apply military pressure on North Vietnam and diplomatic pressure on the Soviet Union.

As regards the Kissinger trip to Moscow, Nixon and Kissinger were agreed about the central strategy. They were both convinced about the importance of keeping up the military pressure on North Vietnam, including the bombing. But there was (again, this was not very common with them) some disagreement about tactics. Nixon wanted Kissinger not only to make Vietnam the first order of business but to refuse to discuss anything that the Soviets wanted, particularly the trade agreements for which they were so eager, until they specifically committed themselves to help end the war. Kissinger pleaded for more flexibility.

A conversation took place at this point which reflects creditably on both Nixon and Kissinger. Kissinger, in Nixon's words, 'perhaps to cheer me up', said that even if the worst happened and the Americans had to pull out in the event of an enemy victory, Nixon would still be able to claim credit for having conducted an honourable winding-down of the war by the dignified and secure withdrawal of 500,000 troops. Nixon refused to be consoled in this comfortable fashion. 'I don't give a damn about the domestic reaction if that happens,' he said, 'because if it does, sitting in this office wouldn't be worth it. The foreign policy of the United States will have been destroyed and the Soviets will have established that they can accomplish what they are after by using the force of arms in Third World countries.' He was as adamant against defeatism as Queen Victoria in the Boer War. He adds, however, in his diary the rueful comment: 'It is ironic that having come this far our fate is really in the hands of the South Vietnamese. If we fail it will be because the American way simply isn't as effective as the Communist way in supporting countries abroad.'

He adds rather touchingly the comment: 'I think perhaps I was too insistent and rough on Henry today ... however when he faces the facts he realizes [? will realize] that no negotiation in Moscow is possible unless we come out all right in Vietnam.' As will be seen in a moment, Nixon came round in the event to Kissinger's standpoint.

The next few weeks are perhaps the most fascinating in the whole story of Nixon's foreign policy. His heart was set on the Moscow summit, but the words of the poet Crosland come to mind:

> I trod the road to hell
> But there were things I might have sold
> And did not sell.

Nothing in the world, certainly no electoral consideration, would have induced Nixon to 'sell' the American prisoners-of-war, or be responsible for denying the South Vietnamese a reasonable chance of survival. He stepped up the bombing, carrying it from the southern part of North Vietnam to the enemy's heartland. On 16 April began a weekend of heavy bombing aimed at destroying the oil depots around Hanoi and Haiphong, which were being used to fuel the invasion. The operation was again a complete military success, but once again the political uproar was deafening.

The day before, however, independently of the bombing, the North Vietnamese had cancelled the Paris talks due for 24 April, at which, according to the Soviet officials, they were supposed to be about to adopt a line of conciliation. Nixon now told Kissinger that he should *not* go to Moscow until it became clear what the Soviet leaders were up to. Kissinger, and it seems Nixon, considered that a crisis of the first magnitude had arisen.

In the afternoon of 15 April Nixon had a grim talk with

Kissinger. He said that what they were really looking at was a cancellation of the summit and 'going hard right on Vietnam, even up to a blockade'. He added the ominous words that, under these circumstances, he had 'an obligation to look for a successor' (presumably when his term as President ran out). Kissinger threw up his hands in horror.

Fortunately, the extreme tension diminished. Kissinger was able to report later that the Soviets were 'desperate' to have him come to Moscow. Nixon agreed that he should go. Nixon's instructions appeared to be fairly definite. Nothing else must be discussed until the Russians agreed to restrain Hanoi. Kissinger seems, however, to have turned a blind eye, in Nelson fashion, to this guidance. The Russians insisted that they had no power to control the North Vietnamese. Kissinger pushed ahead with the other topics and made remarkable progress as Nixon is the first to acknowledge. Brezhnev produced a disarmament proposal that was considerably more favourable than Nixon and Kissinger had expected. Kissinger reported with his usual hyperbole, but there was an element of truth in the message: 'If the summit meeting takes place, you will be able to sign the most important arms control agreement ever concluded.'

Nixon was generous in paying tribute to Kissinger's achievement, though he himself would have risked the loss of the summit for the sake of what he regarded as the only honourable policy in Vietnam. 'In any event', he writes, 'the summit was held, and undoubtedly it owed a large measure of its success to Kissinger's negotiations during this secret visit to Moscow.'

Kissinger met the North Vietnamese on 2 May and reported to Nixon that, after putting up with three hours of insult and invective, he had broken off the talks. When he returned home he felt that there was almost no chance that the Soviet summit would take place. He agreed with Nixon's initial inclination that they should cancel it immediately, in order to prevent the Soviets from doing so first. The arguments on both sides of this question were persuasive. It was hard to see how Nixon could go to the summit and be 'clinking glasses with Brezhnev while Soviet tanks were rumbling through Hue or Quangtri'. On the other hand, to cancel the summit would inevitably be criticized as a hot-headed action inimical to world peace.

After agonizing discussions, not least in his family, Nixon followed a line not so far removed from the advice of John Connally, who recommended: 'The President must not lose the war. And he should not cancel the summit. He's got to show his guts and leadership on this one. Caution be damned – if they cancel, and I don't think they will, we'll ram it right down their throats.' Nixon at this point would seem to have believed that the Russians would in fact cancel the summit. But, undeterred, he went on to deliver a crucial speech on television.

'There is only one way', he said, 'to stop the killing. That is to keep the weapons of war out of the hands of the international outlaws of North Vietnam.' He went on to unfold a programme of drastic measures, beginning with the mining of all entrances to North Vietnamese ports. He then presented a new peace proposal which became the basis for the terms of the final settlement the following January:

First, all American prisoners-of-war must be returned.

Second, there must be an internationally supervised cease-fire throughout Indo-China.

Once prisoners-of-war are released, once the internationally supervised cease-fire has begun, we will stop all acts of force throughout Indo-china, and at that time we will proceed with a complete withdrawal of all American forces from Vietnam within four months.

He concluded with a plea to the Soviet Union, urging them in effect once again to restrain the North Vietnamese: 'Our two nations have made significant progress in our negotiations in recent months.... Let us not slide back toward the dark shadows of a previous age.'

There was the predictable outcry from the critics at home at the mining and other military measures but what really mattered at this point was the response from the Soviet Union. The first official comment was relatively mild. Soon the Russian Ambassador, Dobrynin, was raising procedural questions about the coming summit. So, after all, 'the summit had survived the speech'.

The North Vietnamese attack on the South went on. The American bombing of North Vietnam went on. The plans for the summit went on. This was not quite the summit that Nixon had hoped for, but in retrospect it was vastly better than nothing.

On Saturday 20 May, Nixon and Kissinger and their entourage set off for Moscow via Salzburg. Kissinger exuberantly exclaimed, 'This has to be one of the great diplomatic *coups* of all time. Three weeks ago everyone predicted it would be called off and today we are on our way!' But the other side to that was that the Americans had not in the end insisted on Russian pressure on Hanoi as a condition precedent.

The American guests were welcomed at the airport by President Podgorny. Kosygin and Gromyko were also present. Nixon recalls it as 'a very cool reception'. Soon they were being received by Brezhnev, in the same room as that in which Nixon had first met Khrushchev. Brezhnev's mouth was set in a fixed, rather wary smile. His tone was cordial, but he did not mince matters. He said straight away that he had to tell Nixon that it had not been easy for him to carry off this summit after the recent bombing in Vietnam. 'Only the over-riding importance of improving Soviet-American relations and reaching agreement on some of the serious issues has made it possible.' But he went on to talk more warmly about the necessity and advantages of developing a personal relationship between them.

He made a friendly reference to President Roosevelt. Nixon said that the relationship between Stalin and Roosevelt and Stalin and Churchill supplied a model of the kind of relationship that he would like to have with Brezhnev. 'I would be only too happy, and I am perfectly ready on my side,' Brezhnev replied expansively. 'If we leave all the decisions to the bureaucrats, we will never achieve any progress,' replied Nixon. 'They would simply bury us in paper!' Brezhnev laughed heartily and slapped his palm on the table. It seemed to be a good beginning.

The first plenary session at 11 am next morning, with Brezhnev, Kosygin, Podgorny, Gromyko and Dobrynin, gave Nixon the chance to explain his approach. 'I know', he said, 'that my reputation is one of being a very hard-line, cold-war-orientated anti-communist.' Kosygin said dryly, 'I had heard this some time back.' 'It is true that I have a strong belief in our system', Nixon continued, 'but at the same time I respect those who believe just as strongly in their own systems. There must be room in this world for two great nations with different systems to live together and work together. We cannot do this however by mushy sentimentality or by glossing over differences.' The Soviet leaders nodded, but Nixon guessed that they would have preferred the mushy sentimentality to continue. Still, here he was, their invited guest. Hard bargaining faced them.

Once again no attempt will be made here to describe the social amenities or the diplomatic dialogue in detail. Brezhnev showed extreme friendliness from the beginning, carrying Nixon off unexpectedly to a visit to one of the government *dachas* and taking him for a boat ride on the Moskva river. But at a meeting before dinner, the Soviet leaders denounced him bitterly and emotionally over Vietnam. Brezhnev, who had just been laughing and slapping Nixon on the back, started shouting angrily that instead of honestly working to end the war Nixon was trying to use the Chinese as a means of bringing pressure on the Soviets to intervene with the North Vietnamese. When Brezhnev seemed to have run out of steam, Kosygin and Podgorny carried on the offensive. By this time it was almost eleven o'clock. Nixon replied coolly, but firmly. He had withdrawn over 500,000 men from Vietnam; he had exercised great restraint, but when the North Vietnamese actually invaded South Vietnam he had no choice but to react strongly. 'Our people', he said, 'want peace. I want it too, but I want the Soviet leaders to know how seriously I view this threat of new North Vietnamese escalation.' And he said a good deal more in development of this theme.

Then they went upstairs where a lavish dinner was waiting. Kosygin remarked that it was a good omen for their future relations that, after three hours of the kind of hard-hitting discussions they had just completed, they could still have a relaxed and personally friendly conversation over dinner.

Much later, after Nixon had returned to his room, Kissinger came in, with doubly disquieting news. The Soviets were continuing to hold out for a position unacceptable to the Americans. They were probably hoping that Nixon would be so anxious not to go home without a settlement that at the crunch he would surrender. Worse still, the Pentagon itself was in almost open rebellion and was seeking to repudiate the disarmament concessions previously agreed to. Nixon came out in his best colours at this unpleasant moment. 'To hell with the political consequences,' he said. 'We are going to make an agreement on *our* terms, regardless of the political consequences if the Pentagon won't go along.' 'Just do the best you can', he said to Kissinger, 'and remember that, as far as I am concerned, you don't have to settle this week.' That is how one likes to remember Nixon.

Kissinger's meeting finally broke up in the early morning with the issue still deadlocked, Senator Moynihan, no un-diluted admirer of Kissinger, acknowledges that Kissinger was twice as able as he was because he required half as much sleep. That quality can never have been more valuable than it was on this occasion. On the following day, the news came through that the Politbureau had held a special session and agreed to accept the final American position.

Just after eleven that night in the Kremlin, Brezhnev and Nixon signed the ABM treaty and the Interim Offensive Agreement, thereby establishing a temporary freeze on the numbers of ICBMs and submarine-launched missiles that each side could possess until a permanent agreement was negotiated. *Post tot naufragia portus.* The next day they flew to Leningrad where many thousands who died during the Nazi siege were buried. The young girl acting as guide to Nixon showed him the diary of Tanya, a twelve-year-old girl buried in the cemetery. The diary recorded how, one after another, the members of Tanya's family died. The final entry read: 'All are dead, only Tanya left.' The girl added, choking with emotion, 'Tanya died too.' Nixon wrote in the visitors' book: 'To Tanya and all the heroes of Leningrad.' Next day, in a speech about the dangers of an unchecked arms race, he made use, legitimately and movingly, of his experience the day before.

As we work toward a more peaceful world, let us think of Tanya and of the other Tanyas and their brothers and sisters everywhere.

Let us do all that we can to ensure that no other children will have to endure what Tanya did and that your children and ours, all the children of the world, can live their full lives together in friendship and in peace.

Brezhnev told him after the broadcast that this passage had brought tears to his eyes. Nixon's sentimentality was much derided in sophisticated circles in America, but it was a genuine part of his nature and elicited a genuine response in many lands.

The major achievement of Summit I, as Nixon rightly describes it, was the agreement covering the limitation of strategic arms. The ABM treaty stopped what inevitably would have become a defensive arms race, with untold billions of dollars being spent on each side for more and more ABM coverage. The other major effect of the ABM treaty was to make permanent the concept of deterrence through 'mutual terror'; by giving up missile defences, each side was leaving its population and territory hostage to a strategic missile attack. Each side therefore had an ultimate interest in preventing a war that could only be mutually destructive.

Together with the ABM treaty, the Interim Agreement on strategic missiles marked the first step forward towards arms control in the nuclear age.

A number of other agreements were also signed. Nixon was entitled to see the whole operation and its outcome as the first stage of a far-reaching détente.

Nixon drew further encouragement at the time from a private talk with Brezhnev about Vietnam. Looking back in the light of after-events, it does not seem meaningful.

Nixon's comments on the Russian leaders in his memoirs are worth reading. He records Brezhnev as very warm and friendly. 'As we were leaving in the car out of the dacha, he put his hand on my knee and said he hoped we had developed a good personal relationship.' In the two years that followed, they came nearer and nearer to friendship. Nixon was seldom complacent, certainly not at this time. He had been reading a lot about Yalta. In his eyes, it was not what was agreed to at Yalta that was so disastrous, but the failure of the Soviets to keep the agreement. The major task now was to make sure that the documents which they had just signed took effect in the real world. Nixon is well aware today, and considers that he was aware at the time, that the genuine warm-heartedness of the Russians, including Brezhnev, mitigated in no way the remorselessness of their drive towards world domination.

In *The Real War* (1980), the ex-President indicates a strong practical reason for a strategic arms limitation agreement. He quotes Henry Kissinger's summary:

We needed a freeze, not only for arms control, but for strategic reasons. Our strategy was to agree on a five-year freeze – the interval we judged would enable us to catch up [sic] by developing cruise missiles, a new submarine [Trident], a new ICBM, [MX] and the B-I bomber. ... We froze a disparity which we inherited in order to gain time to reverse the situation. And we did. We stopped no program; we accelerated several....

Elsewhere he points out that, in 1976, two years after he had resigned, it was discovered that American Presidents were being supplied by the CIA with figures on Russian military spending that were only half of what they later decided spending had been. But this does not affect the arguments for the SALT agreement on strategic weapons.

In *The Real War* Nixon warns us of the dangers of a willowy euphoria apt to arise from summitry. He is able to record his televized warning to a joint session of Congress: 'We do not bring back from Moscow the promise of instant peace, but we do bring the beginning of a process that can lead to a lasting peace.' He issued the further caution: 'Soviet ideology still proclaims hostility to some of America's most basic values. The Soviet leaders remain committed to that ideology.' But he candidly admits today that excessive euphoria built up around the 1972 Peking and Moscow summits. 'I must assume', he writes, 'a substantial part of the responsibility for this. It was an election year, and I wanted the political credit for what I believed were genuinely major advances towards a stable peace.'

At home, he found that the Democrats were about to nominate Senator McGovern, a man who had called for unilateral withdrawal from South Vietnam, without any assurances concerning the return of the prisoners-of-war, and proposed crippling reductions in the defence budget. On the face of it a policy so extreme would be rejected by the electorate. The only fear was, from Nixon's point of view, that McGovern would suddenly adjust his policy to make himself respectable. But the chances of a Nixon victory in the presidential elections were now excellent.

On Friday 16 June Nixon conducted a Cabinet meeting and a long session on welfare reform. His schedule ended at 12.45 pm with a posthumous presentation ceremony of the medal of freedom. In the afternoon he left for a weekend in Florida, taking with him a much-read copy of Irvine Kristol's *On the Democratic Idea in America* and a copy of *Triumph and Tragedy*, the last volume of Churchill's world war series, which covers the Yalta conference.

There was never a moment, before or afterwards, when his record seemed more glittering or his prospects more full of promise.

8

The Third-Rate Burglary
17–30 June 1972

And so we come to Watergate. Few Presidents have stood as
high as Nixon after his return from Russia in June 1972. No
President has seemed more sure of triumphant re-election.
No President has ever been dragged lower than Nixon when,
in August 1974, he was driven to resign in order to avoid certain impeachment. His Chief of Staff and other principal aides
were on their way to prison, or there already. The explanation
of this unique catastrophe can be supplied in a single word:
Watergate.

On 27 May 1972 and again on 17 June agents of the Committee for the Re-election of the President broke into the
Democratic National Committee Headquarters in the Watergate, a fashionable hotel, office and apartment complex in
Washington, to install wire-taps and collect other political information. Later Nixon was charged, in the words of the *New
York Times*, '... with having used the office of Presidency
over at least the next two years to conceal the responsibility
of the White House and the re-election committee for the burglaries'. He was never brought to court on this charge
but condemned on it overwhelmingly by public opinion.
No honest person believes that he knew in advance of the
burglaries.

Nixon first heard of the Watergate break-in in prosaic circumstances. On Sunday morning, 18 June, he reached his
house at Key Biscayne from a visit to the Bahamas. He could

106

smell coffee brewing in the kitchen and went in to get a cup. There was a *Miami Herald* on the counter. He glanced over the front page. The main headline was about the Vietnam withdrawal. There was a small story in the middle of the page on the left-hand side. It appeared that five men, four of them from Miami, had been arrested in the Democratic National Committee HQ, at the Watergate in Washington. It appeared that one of the five men had identified himself as a former employee of the CIA; three of the others were Cuban natives. They had all been wearing rubber surgical gloves. 'It sounded preposterous,' writes Nixon. 'Cubans in surgical gloves bugging the DNC. I dismissed it as some sort of prank.' He rang Bob Haldeman and twice during the day rang Colson without apparently asking him about the break-in. At that point it did not seem worth his discussing it.

On Monday morning the Watergate break-in was still the furthest thing from his mind. He talked on the telephone to Colson and a number of others, including his daughter and Billy Graham. He made two short calls to Haldeman who then came over for an hour's discussion, but by Monday night Watergate had come into his diary. On the way back to Washington in the aeroplane, 'I got the disturbing news from Bob Haldeman that the break-in at the Democratic National Committee involved someone who was on the payroll of the committee to re-elect the President [CRP].' Mitchell had told Haldeman on the phone 'enigmatically, not to get involved in it'. Nixon told Haldeman 'that I simply hoped that none of our people were involved for two reasons – one, because it was stupid in the way it was handled, and two, because I could see no reason whatever for trying to bug the National Committee'.

But meanwhile the story of Watergate, which only reached the President second- or third-hand, was going forward apace. Once again we must retrace our steps. On 3 December 1971 a certain Gordon Liddy, a former CIA agent, later to be described by Nixon not unfairly as 'a nut case', was brought to a certain Jeb Magruder by a certain John Dean. Dean was at that time aged thirty-one, the personal legal adviser to the President. He was very smooth, very good-looking and, as he tells us in his revealing book, full of 'blind ambition'.

Magruder, not much older, also smooth and good-looking, but a more attractive figure to the reader, had been a cosmetic salesman in California and discovered by Haldeman. He was acting head of the campaign for the re-election of the President. The heavy responsibilities placed on these young men were regretted by all concerned afterwards. The intended head of the campaign for the re-election was John Mitchell, close friend and law partner of the President, who had become Attorney-General at his urgent wish and who was now ceasing to hold that office to handle the re-election campaign. His glamorous but unbalanced wife was placing a great strain on his nerves. Throughout this crucial period he was incapable of performing the tasks allotted to him. He was never quite sure whether his wife would still be alive from one minute to another.

No student of Watergate can pass over Mitchell too lightly. Bill Safire, one of Nixon's three superlative speech writers, the others being Ray Price and Pat Buchanan, devotes two chapters to Mitchell. In his book *Before the Fall*, which is indispensable reading, he presents a moving portrait. 'Picture a natural athlete who, in his youth, moonlighted by playing semi-pro hockey, the roughest, fastest sport of all; picture the same man in World War II a born leader, a navy commander choosing a command in the highest risk, most daring and exciting branch of the navy. Picture him in middle-age, still the most hopeless romantic, choosing to marry an unstable, glamorous Southern belle, resolutely sticking by her against all prudence until she left him, because as he kept putting it to cynical questioners "I love her.".' These qualities, Safire tells us, belonged to the sour, pipe-sucking, blood-hound-visaged 'heavy' of the Nixon administration, Nixon's first Attorney-General.

In 1973 he lost it all: his wife, his reputation for integrity, his cool, his money, his future, retaining only – and in heightened form – 'his public image as an unfeeling, heavy-lidded villain, dedicated only to the success of Richard Nixon'. But this is a book about Nixon, not Mitchell, though such a book would be well worth writing.

'Jeb,' said Dean to Magruder, 'the Attorney-General Mitchell thinks Gordon [Liddy] is the ideal man to be your general counsellor.' Liddy, a lawyer, is revealed in his memoirs as the eccentric to end eccentrics. Soon he was asking for a million dollars.

A meeting took place in Mitchell's room. Mitchell, Magruder, Liddy and Dean were present. Liddy's plans included mugging squads, kidnapping, sabotage, the use of prostitutes for political blackmail, break-ins to obtain and photograph documents and various forms of electronic surveillance and wire-tapping. Mitchell puffed on his pipe; 'Gordon,' he said, 'That is not quite what we had in mind and the money you are asking for is way out of line. Why don't you tone it down a little, then we will talk about it again.' Liddy was stunned at Mitchell's disapproval. He agreed to present a new version. Magruder called Gordon Strachan, assistant to Haldeman, and outlined Liddy's proposal for him to pass on to Haldeman. This, however, does not appear to have been done.

On 4 February a second meeting with Mitchell took place. A reduced plan was submitted. The meeting ended with the second Liddy plan still dangling. Dean at one point said, 'I think it is inappropriate for this to be discussed with the Attorney-General. I think that in the future Gordon [Liddy] should discuss his plans with Jeb, then Jeb can pass them on to the Attorney-General.' A long delay followed of about two months before the third meeting on Liddy's plan. Mitchell was increasingly preoccupied with the Senate inquiry. He was about to resign as Attorney-General to become full-time campaign director. Liddy apparently complained to Colson about the delay. Colson telephoned Magruder: 'Why don't you guys get off the stick and get Liddy's budget approved?' Apparently he said that the White House needed the information, particularly information about O'Brien, the chairman of the Democratic Party. But Colson, who has made many damaging admissions in his book, insists that he did not know that the latest Liddy budget included a break-in. I believe him. Liddy, in any case, teamed up with a little-known ex-CIA agent Hunt who, as we have already seen, had been involved with him in the earlier break-in at Ellsberg's psychiatrist's office.

On 29 March Magruder saw Mitchell at the Key Biscayne

Hotel. Many points were dealt with. Finally they came to the Liddy espionage plan. 'All of us', writes Magruder, 'expressed doubts. We feared that it might be a waste of money and might be dangerous, but we were all persuaded of Liddy's competence and we all knew of the atmosphere [*sic*] at the White House.' He assumed that Haldeman wanted it because he had asked if Strachan had any comments to make and Strachan had replied that the plan was all right with Haldeman if it was all right with Mitchell.

Finally Mitchell told Magruder that he approved the plan. Liddy should receive 250,000 dollars. 'Some of our opponents used illegal means to achieve the end' (Magruder). I have relied considerably above on Magruder's version but I do not believe that in fact Haldeman had approved the break-in plan, let alone Colson and least of all the President.

Mitchell has always denied that he himself ever approved the plan. Myself, I cannot but believe that he did approve it, in the sense of allowing Magruder to go ahead, but carelessly, it may well be, without bringing his mind to bear on its real character. Later a number of leading officials including Mitchell, Haldeman, Ehrlichman, Magruder and Dean were convicted of offences in connection with the cover-up. But no one except the original seven, that is the five burglars plus Liddy and Hunt, were ever charged with the responsibility for the burglary itself.

We move on to 18 June. Magruder was having breakfast in the Polo Lounge of the Beverley Hills Hotel, Los Angeles, when he received a telephone call from Liddy. The news was fairly shattering: 'Our security chief [Jim McCord] was arrested in the Democratic Headquarters last night.' Liddy tried to reassure him: 'The four men arrested with McCord were Cuban freedom fighters whom Howard Hunt recruited. But don't worry; my man will never talk.' Magruder had an instinct that something frightful had happened. 'Oh God!' he moaned, 'why didn't I fire that idiot Liddy when I had the chance? How could we have been so stupid!' Magruder then saw Mitchell. They both agreed that McCord was the heart of the problem. 'It did not seem beyond our capacity to get our man out of the jail.' Later Liddy reported that he had approached the new Attorney-General, but that the latter had refused to talk to him about freeing McCord. The *Washington Post* carried a brief story by two reporters 'we had never heard of' – Bernstein and Woodward. 'Two men, one of whom said he was a former employee of the Central Intelligence Agency, were arrested at 2.30 am yesterday in what authorities described as an elaborate plot to bug the offices of the Democratic National Committee here.' But they were still being very cautious. The story went on: 'There was no immediate explanation as to why the five suspects would want to bug the Democratic National Committee offices, or whether or not they were working for any other individuals or organizations.'

The writing on the wall was plain enough for Magruder and his colleagues. 'My life', he writes, 'changed that day. For the first time I realized that we were involved in criminal activity. That if the truth became known we would all go to jail. The cover-up was immediate and automatic. It seemed inconceivable that with our political power we could not erase the mistake.' It is worth noticing that when Haldeman describes the subsequent meeting with Nixon on 23 June, he treats Nixon as involved in the cover-up from then onwards. But he insists that neither Nixon nor himself looked upon it as criminal at that time. In 1977, Nixon was still insisting to David Frost that a sharp line had to be drawn between a legal and an illegal cover-up. Of course Mitchell and Magruder were much more vulnerable as they had approved of and sponsored the break-in, itself a criminal action.

Next morning Haldeman rang Magruder. He summoned him to Washington, 'to take charge of the cover-up' in Magruder's phrase. One can't accept these as Haldeman's words, but the request to return to Washington was undeniable. Magruder, in his own account, 'spoke with the assumption that Haldeman knew about the break-in plan'. He was too frightened to tell Haldeman that the plan had in fact been approved by Mitchell and himself. Haldeman still insists that he himself knew nothing about it in advance.

The first person Magruder met in his office was Sloane, the treasurer of the campaign fund. Sloane brought the unwelcome tidings that the money found on the burglars was money he himself had given to Liddy and that 'it could probably be traced to us'. Liddy came in very downcast. 'It looks like we have got a problem Gordon,' said Magruder, with considerable understatement. 'Yeah,' admitted Liddy, 'I goofed.' It is almost incredible that such an experienced little group should have made such a mess of it all. Many suspicions have been aroused accordingly, but nothing has been proved.

A meeting followed in Mitchell's office. Mitchell and the others were all bitter and disillusioned. Various arrangements were made to destroy incriminating documents. Once the leaders of CRP denied any involvement in the Watergate, it became necessary, says Magruder, 'to develop a complicated cover story that would place the full blame on Gordon Liddy and show that he had misappropriated for his own illegitimate ends money that we had given him for legitimate purposes'. The basic goal of the cover story was to make Liddy solely responsible for the break-in. It was assumed that Liddy, Hunt and McCord would keep silent about the break-in having been approved by Mitchell. 'Our all-consuming fear was that if the blame moved past Liddy, it would swiftly reach the President himself and endanger his re-election.'

The basic problem in the first week concerned the money authorized for Liddy. They would not try to conceal the fact that they had authorized $250,000 to Liddy for intelligence-gathering operations. They did have to work out ways of making it appear that the authorized operations were legitimate. Before President Nixon was ever personally involved, a break-in unauthorized by him had taken place and plans had been formulated to conceal the responsibility for this criminal action.

We return to Nixon. On Tuesday morning, 20 June, his first day back in Washington, there was what he calls 'a new twist' to the story. A front-page headline in the *Washington Post* proclaimed: 'White House consultant tied to bugging figure.' The name of Howard Hunt had been found in the address books of two of the men found inside the DNC headquarters. In fact Woodward had received a call at home late at night from Eugene Bachinski, the *Washington Post* regular night police reporter. The Miami suspects' belongings were listed in a confidential police inventory that Bachinski had obtained. There were 'two pieces of yellow-lined paper, one addressed to "Dear friend Mr Howard" and another to "Dear Mr H.H."' and an unmailed envelope containing Hunt's personal check for $6.36 made out to the Lakewood Country Club in Rockville along with a bill for the same amount. The *Washington Post* stated that, until the end of March 1972, Hunt, a former CIA agent, had worked at the White House as a consultant to Chuck Colson (this was not accurate). Nixon was now seriously disturbed. Colson was a member of his inner circle of aides and advisors. If he was drawn in, it would be 'a whole new situation'. Nixon had always valued Colson's 'hardball instincts' and encouraged him to give full rein to them. Had he gone too far this time?

Meanwhile, the Democratic Party were already mounting an attack. They had filed a million-dollar suit against the CRP for invasion of privacy and violation of civil rights. They would have an opportunity in this way to ask probing questions about any and every aspect of the Republican campaign.

At 2.20 pm Colson came in to see the President. He took a very reassuring line. He explained the presence of Hunt's name in the address books of the arrested men on the grounds that they all had CIA ties. Hunt had trained Cuban exiles for the Bay of Pigs operation. This seemed to reinforce the notion that it was a Cuban operation. Nixon did what he could to cheer up Colson, who seemed cheerful enough when he left. He said that he would love to have depositions taken from the White House staff, because 'everyone is completely out of it ... this is once when you'd like for people to testify'. He said it with complete conviction. Nixon hoped that it was true.

He saw Haldeman before and after the meeting with Colson, the first meeting lasting an hour and twenty minutes and the second less than an hour. In Nixon's words 'what was said during the morning [20 June] meeting will never be known completely'.

Haldeman in his book offers a speculative reconstruction of what was said. 'I wonder', he writes, 'if one of my conversations with Nixon about Colson didn't take place 20 June. With that thought in mind, I've reconstructed the way the conversation might have gone.' But this is not how history can be written and Haldeman now disavows it. Nixon himself suggests that the conversation in the morning can be more authentically reconstructed from the afternoon's discussion which was recorded on tape. In the afternoon Haldeman said that he did not think that Colson had known specifically that the Watergate bugging project was under way, nor did he think that John Mitchell had known beforehand about it. He admitted, however, that there was clearly going to be an effort to tie Mitchell in and, for that matter, Colson. 'Our people were making an effort to keep the incident tied to the motive of Cuban nationalism.'

Nixon seemed fairly happy as the day's work ended. 'As I walked back to the residence that night I felt comforted.' He telephoned John Mitchell. According to Nixon's diary, Mitchell was 'terribly chagrined that the activities of anybody attached to his committee should have been handled in such a manner', and he only regretted that he had 'not policed all the people more effectively . . . in his own organization'. Later Nixon telephoned Haldeman. He told him about a new idea for handling the public-relations aspect of the Watergate incident, laying more and more stress on the 'Cuban explanation'. Haldeman in his book suggests that this telephone conversation proves that by the evening of 20 June Nixon was already deeply involved in plans for a cover-up. But Nixon closed his diary for the day with this note: 'I felt better today than I have really for months – relaxed and was able to do more work than even we usually do with far more enthusiasm.' In his memoirs he sums up his attitude at that time as follows: 'Watergate was an annoying problem, but it was still just a minor one among many.' He was certainly not conscious of being involved in a conspiracy.

21 June and 22 June can be seen as a prelude to the fatal 23 June. On the 21st Haldeman told Nixon that 'Gordon Liddy was the guy who did this'. Nixon had no idea up till then who Liddy was. He was still taking it fairly lightly. He said that if someone asked him about Press Secretary Ziegler's statement that it was a third-rate burglary, he was going to say that 'it was only a third-rate attempt at a burglary'.

Haldeman told him that the lawyers all felt that if Liddy

and the arrested men entered a guilty plea, they would only get fines and suspended sentences. Apparently they were all first offenders. It is amazing to recall that, in the event, they were initially given sentences of thirty-five to forty years, with the evident intention of making them 'spill the beans'.

Nixon was still worried about Mitchell. If Mitchell were involved, there would be a real problem and he was not prepared in that case for a policy of complete candour. Haldeman, who had been so confident that Mitchell was not involved, was now less sure. Nixon by his own account 'still believed that Mitchell was innocent'. He felt sure that he would not have been involved in something so stupid. But he adds that he 'never personally confronted Mitchell with the direct question of whether he had been involved or had known about the planning of the Watergate break-in. He was one of my closest friends and he had issued a public denial.'

Nixon cannot avoid severe criticism on this point. But fidelity to friends is not a contemptible quality. Most of us prefer leaders who are faithful to their friends – Churchill, for example – to those who have no such feeling.

But Mitchell, by this time it was clear, was not the whole problem. Haldeman was concerned about what he called 'other involvements' – facts that an investigative fishing expedition could uncover and exploit politically. The Democrats were bringing a civil suit which could produce a lot of unwelcome information. No one seemed to be quite sure what Colson had or had not done, apart from Watergate where he did seem to be completely in the clear.

On 22 June there was a press conference in the afternoon. Nixon was prepared to say that no one in the White House had been involved in the break-in and that he 'absolutely believed John Mitchell's statement denying that he had known anything about it'. He was certainly convinced that what he was saying was true at the time.

Now comes 23 June, *dies irae*. It is conceivable that if the crucial conversation with Haldeman had not taken place on this day Nixon might have survived as President. Certainly, the Republicans who defended him stoutly against impeachment on the judicial committee of the House of

Representatives had to admit in the end that it was impossible to resist impeachment once the information about 23 June emerged from the tape.

The minority group voted against the articles of impeachment when the vote was taken in the House of Representatives but that was before the tapes of the 23 June meeting became available. After they were published they were driven to admit the President's guilt in respect of one impeachable offence – obstruction of justice in connection with the Watergate investigation. One Congressman added a closely reasoned expression of his individual views. He agreed that in the light of the 23 June 1972 conversations it was impossible to continue to defend the President. But he boldly suggests that 'even the evidence set forth above would not have greatly disturbed the Congress or the country had it been disclosed in the spring of 1973.' The damage was done by the apparent policy of the President to withhold until he finally was forced to yield information which, because of the timing of disclosure, put him in the worst possible light.

The Congressman ended with the reflection, 'History will deal more kindly with Richard Nixon than did his contemporaries.' As the Watergate affair moves into the past, 'it may be seen for what a little thing a President was forced to resign from office when compared with the accomplishments of his administration. A legal case of obstruction of justice was made against him. But instructions by other Presidents had undoubtedly altered the course of other investigations without controversy.' The abuses of power charged against the President were probably no greater than have occurred in some other administrations. Historically, therefore, the six-minute discussion of Watergate which took place between Nixon and Haldeman on 23 June 1972 in the course of a ninety-minute conversation was fatal to Nixon. What was said that inflicted so mortal a wound when it came to light?

Haldeman began by telling Nixon that the news was far from good: the FBI was not under control because Acting Director Pat Gray did not know how to control it and the investigation was leading into some productive areas. In particular the FBI was apparently going to be able to trace the money after all. 'And it goes in some direction we don't want

it to go,' Haldeman said. Unless they could find some way
to limit the investigation the trail would lead directly to the
CRP, and their political containment would go by the board.
Haldeman said that Mitchell and John Dean had come up
with an idea as to how to deal with the problem.

Now comes the crucial quotation from Nixon's memoirs:
'As Haldeman explained it, General Vernon Walters, the
Deputy Director of the CIA, was to call Pat Gray and tell him
"to stay the hell out of this ... business. We don't want you
to come any further on it.".' Nixon assented. In his own
account he did not want Haldeman to lie and say there was
no involvement. 'I wanted him to set out the situation in such
a way that Helms and Walters [Director and Deputy Director
of the CIA] would take the initiative and go to the FBI on their
own.'

Well, there it is. That is what Nixon agreed to. He wanted
what he still regarded as a 'sort of Comedy of Errors' to be
covered up in the interests of himself, no doubt, but also of
the Presidency, and the country and the world causes to which
he was dedicated – not to mention his friends and subordi-
nates. But in a long conversation only six minutes were spent
on that topic. The move in any case led nowhere. It is perfectly
credible that he (Nixon) had little recollection of the discussion afterwards.

During the remaining few days in June, when Nixon discussed the Watergate break-in, it was in his own words
'mainly to express my irritation that nothing seemed to be
happening to settle the case and remove it from the public
eye'. On 26 June, he was asking Haldeman if there was any
way to get the people involved to plead guilty. Haldeman told
him that guilty pleas would have to await the indictments and
the indictments were being delayed, because the FBI had kept
investigating 'and uncovering new things'. There was the
complication that the men involved in the Watergate bugging
had also been involved in 'standard intelligence and political
projects'. Nixon still clung to the idea of Mitchell's innocence.

On 28 June he was saying to Haldeman that, as he understood it, Mitchell had not known specifically about the bugging. Haldeman answered that, as he understood it, that was
correct. On 30 June, the news was not too good. There was

a newspaper story that Howard Hunt's safe at the White House had been opened and various things had been discovered, including an unloaded gun. Haldeman said that 'some other things in the safe had been handled at a high discreet level in the Bureau'. Nixon did not enquire further. He was surprised that Hunt had a safe at the White House, as he had apparently not worked there for several months. Haldeman told him that the things in question had simply been left behind.

Nixon was disappointed to learn that the FBI were still 'going after Hunt'. He had thought that 'they were going to keep away from him as a result of Haldeman's meeting with Helms and Walters of the CIA'. He was told that these efforts had been unproductive. Later in the day Haldeman told him that Liddy was going to write a scenario that would tie together all the loose ends. He would take the responsibility for planning the entire Watergate operation and say that no one higher up had authorized it. Obviously this scenario made sense and was not altogether dishonest in view of the fact that Liddy had originated the whole disastrous move and had been in charge throughout. Nixon expressed, no doubt genuinely, serious concern about Liddy's family. He still was looking on Watergate as 'a ridiculous goddam thing'.

He tells us in his memoirs that his extensive diary notes from 21 June to 30 June are predominantly about foreign policy, domestic issues, campaign planning and personal and family observations. Watergate still loomed very small. But on 30 June, the night before he left for California, he dictated a brief reflection about the position:

Diary
The major problem on the Watergate is simply to clean the thing up by having whoever was responsible admit what happened. Certainly I am satisfied that nobody in the White House had any knowledge or approved any such activity, and that Mitchell was not aware of it as well.

Yet insensibly he was crossing a calamitous Rubicon. 'It was in these days,' he writes, 'at the end of June and the beginning of July 1972 that I took the first steps down the road that eventually led to the end of my Presidency.' He did nothing to discourage the various stories which were being considered to explain the break-in, stories which he knew to be at least partially untrue. He approved efforts 'to encourage the CIA to intervene and limit the FBI investigation'. It was his approval of these efforts which was to bring about his ruin.

Later he goes on: 'My actions and inactions would appear to many as part of a widespread and conscious cover-up.' He did not see them as such; he was handling in his own eyes 'in a pragmatic way what I perceived as an annoying and strictly political problem. I was looking for a way to deal with Watergate that would minimize the damage to me and my friends and my campaign, while giving the least advantage to my political opposition. I saw Watergate as politics pure and simple.'

9
Fleeting Triumph
July–December 1972

From 1 July to the end of the year Watergate was a minor anxiety for Nixon, though it could never be neglected in its bearing on the election. We will come back to it shortly, but it occupied only a few pages in Nixon's memoirs from July to December. The two outstanding concerns were his re-election campaign and Vietnam. The first he found surprisingly dull and unexciting. This presidential election should have been, he writes, the most gratifying and fulfilling of all his campaigns. 'Instead, it was one of the most frustrating and, in many ways, the least satisfying of all.' This, in spite of the triumphant result. The explanation cannot be found in Watergate. He had assumed that his opponent would be Kennedy, Muskie or Humphrey. He had expected a hard battle for re-election. When McGovern was selected, he felt like a man in a tug-of-war whose opponent has let go of the rope. He accepted the fact that he was virtually assured of re-election without having to wage much of a campaign. His adrenalin failed to flow. His zest was much diminished.

There is no need to dwell on the details of the campaign, though Nixon's side of it was acknowledged to be exceptionally efficient. Two anecdotes are worth re-telling. L.B.J. sent him some campaign advice through Billy Graham. 'Ignore McGovern and get out with the people. But stay above the campaign, like I did with Goldwater. Go to ball games and factories. And don't worry. The McGovern people are going to defeat themselves.' What followed has an ironical interest. Billy Graham said that when he had raised the question of the Watergate bugging business, Johnson had just laughed and said, 'Hell, that's not going to hurt him a bit,' – an expert opinion that turned out woefully wrong.

The other anecdote will appeal to anyone who is not hopelessly biased against Nixon. The Democratic candidate for Vice-President, Thomas Eagleton, was compelled to drop off the ticket when it was discovered that he had had psychiatric treatment, including shock therapy. Nixon thought immediately of Eagleton's family: 'I knew their agony must have been like that we had suffered during the Fund crisis.' That had a happy ending. Nixon remembered that Eagleton had brought his young son to the Oval Office the year before. He sat down and wrote him a letter which included these passages: 'What matters is not that your father fought a terribly difficult battle and lost. What matters is that in fighting the battle he won the admiration of foes and friends alike because of the courage, pains and just plain guts he showed against overwhelming odds. . . . Years later you will look back and say, "I am proud of the way my Dad handled himself in the greatest trial of his life.".' Even Lincoln, who wrote many moving letters of sympathy, could not have improved on that one. Terry Eagleton, aged thirteen, was fully equal to the occasion. 'I guess very few thirteen-year-olds get handwritten letters from the president. Although I am a Democrat, I think you must be a wonderful man to take the time to write to some unimportant person like me. . . . My favourite subject in school is history. I now feel I am a part of history since you wrote a letter to me. Thank you, Mr President, very, very much. With appreciation, Terry Eagleton.'

The Vietnam front at last saw positive movement. Kissinger had been negotiating more or less secretly with the North Vietnamese for three years. In August 1972 the latter seemed at last to realize that the mass of American opinion was firmly behind the hard line adopted by Nixon. On 12 October Kissinger told Nixon that at last he saw prospects of successful negotiation. The North Vietnamese had made confidential proposals that went a long way to accepting the American position. Nixon quickly replied that a basis now appeared to exist for an agreement ending the war and restoring peace in Vietnam, though there were still technical issues to be discussed. It seemed that the North Vietnamese were anxious for a settlement before the election on the assumption that a victorious Nixon would be still tougher to deal with afterwards.

But difficulties arose with South Vietnam and also with the North. Kissinger made his first appearance on national television on 26 October. 'The White House public relations people had hitherto been convinced', he writes, 'that my accent might disturb Middle America; they therefore permitted pictures but no sound at my "on the record" press conferences.' On 26 October they finally took a chance on Kissinger's pronunciation. Afterwards no doubt they regretted their magnanimity. He used the expression: 'We believe that peace is at hand.' He still claims that the statement was essentially true, though much opprobrium was heaped on him when it took another three months to make it effective. The election arrived on 7 November with peace still in the balance.

Contrary to what is usually supposed, Nixon was not pressing Kissinger for a peace announcement before the election. Colson recalls that he had in mind the example of Churchill who 'won the war and was immediately hurled from office'.

John Mitchell was still desperately concerned with his erratic wife. She at least provided him with a genuine excuse for resigning as campaign manager. Nixon refers to him as 'one of my few personal friends', and adds the comment, 'Without Martha, I am sure that the Watergate thing would never have happened.' When there was news about Watergate, it was nearly always bad. Nixon learned early in July from Gray, the new, still unconfirmed director of the FBI, that he was upset about what he saw as attempts on the part of the White House to frustrate the FBI's inquiry. Nixon had understood – an important statement this – that Gray had actually wanted help from Walters of the CIA in controlling an investigation that he agreed was getting out of hand. But now he told Gray emphatically to go ahead with his full investigation. He told Ehrlichman 'to be sure that both Helms at the CIA and Gray at the FBI knew that I wanted a full investigation and that we were not attempting to suppress anything'. All this must be accepted as genuine proof that from July onwards Nixon gave the 'all clear' to the law-enforcement authorities. It could be said cynically that the other route had failed. But the cynic does not always present the whole truth.

On 8 July Ehrlichman went for a walk with Nixon on 'a beautiful California day on the beach'. It was now becoming clear that Jeb Magruder, deputy head of the CRP, was deeply involved. The question of clemency for Magruder, Hunt, Liddy and the five defendants cropped up. Nixon and Ehrlichman agreed that there should be no commitments of any kind on clemency at that time. It was recognized, however, that there were precedents for pardons of political offences. When Truman became President, dozens of his fellow Democratic workers had been convicted of fraud in the 1936 elections. Truman began pardoning them before he had been in office a month. Any decision would have to be made later regarding the Watergate delinquents. 'If', wrote Nixon in his diary, 'there were equivalent defences on both sides, that would provide the necessary basis for pardoning the individuals involved in this caper.'

29 August saw Nixon's first press conference of the campaign. He was still assured by all his advisers that there was no White House involvement in Watergate. He was asked at the press conference whether he would appoint a special prosecutor. He replied that a special prosecutor was hardly necessary since the FBI, the Justice Department, the Senate Banking and Currency Committee and the General Accounting Office were all conducting investigations. He had ordered total co-operation by the White House. In addition to that, within his own staff, under his direction, counsel to the President Mr Dean had conducted a complete investigation of all leads which might involve any present members of the White House staff or anybody in the government. He could say categorically that his investigation indicated that no one on the White House staff, no one in this administration, presently employed, was involved in this very bizarre incident. . . . 'What really hurts in matters of this sort is not the fact that they occur, because over-zealous people in campaigns do things

that are wrong; what really hurts is if you try to cover it up.'

He certainly believed it to be true. He was not conscious of authorizing any illegality. But meanwhile he was relying on Dean and others to 'contain the political damage' – a nice distinction which, in retrospect, seems more unreal than occurred to anyone at the time.

The Attorney-General on 12 September was able to report that, in spite of the biggest investigation of the FBI since the Kennedy assassination, no one in the White House would be indicted. When in fact the indictments were handed down on 15 September, only Hunt, Liddy and the five men arrested in the Democratic headquarters were named. Nixon's diary for that day indicated the relative unimportance still attributed to Watergate. In a long talk with Dean, he thanked him for his work. He said to him, 'So you just try to button it up as well as you can and hope for the best. And remember that basically the damn thing is just one of those unfortunate things and we are trying to cut our losses.' Later he commented, 'I had a good talk with John Dean and was enormously impressed with him.'

Meanwhile Woodward and Bernstein (of the *Washington Post*) were beavering away without undue scrupulosity. 'The trick was getting inside someone's apartment or house. There a conversation could be pursued, consciences could be appealed to, the reporters could try to establish themselves as human beings.' The approaches that seemed to work best were certainly less than straightforward.

If they had confined themselves to their first book, they might have gone down in history as knights in shining armour. Attorney-General Richard Kleindienst said that the indictments represented the culmination of 'one of the most intensive, objective and thorough investigations in many years, reaching out to cities all across the United States, as well as into foreign countries'. But at the *Washington Post* Bernstein, Woodward and the editors had become increasingly sceptical of the whole federal investigation. Various sums of money were not mentioned in the indictment which the *Post* was following up intensively. How could the indictment be so limited if the government had the same information as the *Post*? By the end of September they were hot on the trail of John Mitchell and publishing damaging innuendoes. Mitchell was naturally furious. Bernstein rang him at 11.30 one evening and addressed him thus over the telephone:

BERNSTEIN [after identifying himself]: Sir, I'm sorry to bother you at this hour, but we are running a story in tomorrow's paper that, in effect, says that you controlled secret funds at the committee while you were Attorney-General.
MITCHELL: Jeeeeeeeeeesus! You said that? What does it say?
BERNSTEIN: I'll read you the first few paragraphs. [He got as far as the third, Mitchell responding 'Jeeeeeeeeesus' every few words.]
MITCHELL: All that crap, you're putting it in the paper? It's all been denied. Katie Graham's gonna get her tit caught in a big fat wringer if that's published. Good Christ! That's the most sickening thing I ever heard.

In October McGovern, the Democratic candidate, who was by this time clearly losing, began to focus on corruption in government. Unfortunately for Nixon a young man called Donald Segretti had been employed by Dwight Chapin, Nixon's appointments secretary, and Gordon Strachan, an aide to Haldeman, to become what they called 'a Republican Dick Tuck' (all this unknown to Nixon). Tuck was a Democrat notorious for ingenious 'gags' aimed at Republican candidates. He was a master of so-called 'dirty tricks', planting embarrassing signs in campaign crowds, changing schedules in order to create confusion and generally spreading disruption. Segretti, like Tuck, was supposed to 'use his imagination and his sense of humour', to cause minor disarray among the opposition. Unfortunately he went altogether too far and was duly apprehended. There was no real connection with Watergate, though that with Haldeman was difficult to explain away. The outcry was vociferous.

But the public were not in a mood to be deflected from their determination to see Nixon re-elected. Even the *Washington Post* had more or less dropped Watergate by the time of the election. Nixon was returned on 7 November with a spanking majority. He received 60.7 per cent of the votes to 37.5 per cent. This was the second largest percentage of the popular vote in the history of American politics and the greatest ever given to a Republican candidate. Only Lyndon Johnson, running against Goldwater in the unique circumstances of 1964, had received fractionally more: 01.1 per cent. Nixon received the largest number of popular votes ever cast for a presidential candidate and the second largest number of electoral votes. No Presidential candidate ever won so many states.

Nixon recalls an inexplicable melancholy that settled over him on that victorious night. To some extent he admits that Watergate may have played a part. If so, it was only 'one of a number of factors'. But soon he recovered. He was confident that a new era was about to begin. 'And I was eager to begin it.'

Nixon records that his first priority was to end the war. It will be seen in a moment that this was not achieved until the end of January. Meanwhile a large part of his mind was given to far-reaching plans for a profound reorganization of American government. Since in the event these plans came to nothing, they have today a poignant, almost macabre interest. He had three main areas of reform for his second term: (1) to reform the budget and terminate wasteful and ineffective programmes; (2) to bring about a massive reorganization and reduction of the federal bureaucracy and White House staff; (3) to revitalize the Republican party along the lines of a new majority which in his view had emerged during the election. He had no illusions, he writes today, about the reactions such reforms would provoke from the bureaucracy and Congress and the media. 'But I was ready, willing and I felt able to do battle for them because I believed in them and because I believed they were the right things for America.' His sheer audacity takes one's breath away as one reads. In his eyes the Democrats held all four aces in Washington: the Congress, the bureaucracy, the majority of the media and the formidable group of lawyers and power-brokers who operated behind the scenes. By British standards it would be suicidal for any single leader to tackle head-on this vast array of opponents. But Nixon quotes with approval a columnist who said of him later, 'What Richard Nixon contemplated doing was actually running the government. Something no president in seven decades had attempted.'

The British reader, however, may go wrong here in assessing one aspect of Nixon's proposed reconstruction. He may assume that an attempt by the President to extend his control of the executive is similar to a British Prime Minister's ambitions in the same direction. But, in the British case, the Prime Minister would be enlarging his own role at the expense of his Ministers. In Nixon's case, the President is the supreme head of the executive and is fully entitled to make his will prevail, so long as he does not tamper with Congress or the judiciary.

In a broader sense, Nixon had just achieved a tremendous victory in the face of all his deeply entrenched opponents. He meant to exploit it to the full in the interests, as he saw it, not of himself as an individual but of a nobler, more patriotic kind of America. He set to work to reorganize the Cabinet immediately.

Theodore White writes of Nixon's proposed reorganization after the 1972 triumph: 'Theoretically much of the idea *did* make sense; government in Washington is smothered and embalmed in regulations.' He quotes one senior civil servant as he reflected on the scheme later: 'Our system of government is really, truly at the point of breakdown. The trouble is that Richard Nixon thought he could solve the problem by putting "sons-of-bitches" in command.'

But 'Teddy' White is not quite consistent in his attitude to the Nixon entourage. Elsewhere in his book he pays tribute to the genuine American patriotism, misguided though it proved, of Haldeman, Ehrlichman and others. He brings out, however, more than one vital point under-emphasized by other writers – for example, the unforeseen deterioration of the economic situation from 1973 onwards. The year 1972, as he points out, had been one of the greatest years of American economic history: there had been a boom larger and more fairly distributed to ordinary people than the boom of 1929. And he continues: 'It would be entirely unfair to blame Richard Nixon for the disaster which was now about to happen to the American money system in the next year, or the crisis of confidence in all values which was about to take place in the next two years.' If anyone could have given him the right advice there is reason to suppose he would have taken it. But no one could. A Marxist, which I am not, would find here an obvious explanation of the Watergate disaster to follow. Without being a Marxist one can feel that the economic deterioration was to play no small part in the general loss of confidence in the President.

Colson gives a vivid account of the atmosphere at the Republican headquarters after Nixon's landslide victory. 'I stood there thinking that, unlike any celebration I had attended in twenty years in politics, there was no air of triumph here. The faces before us were unsmiling, looking in fact disappointed and even imposed upon. Around big boards, where the continuing returns were posting record-breaking margins for Nixon, there was scarcely a ripple of excitement.'

Then came the summons to the President. Haldeman was sitting at a small antique table, poring over election returns. He never looked up as Colson walked in: 'Sit down, Chuck, and have a drink with me,' said the President. Haldeman never drank. Colson supposed that Nixon had been anxiously awaiting his arrival. 'Here's to you Chuck. Those are your votes that are pouring in.' But Haldeman's grimness spread to Colson. 'What's wrong, Chuck?' asked Nixon. 'Why aren't you smiling and celebrating?' 'I guess I am a bit numb,' said Colson. Nixon, who always found it hard to show his emotions managed to blurt out: 'I just want you to know I'll always be grateful,' and so the night ended tamely.

The next morning Colson was summoned early to a meeting of the assembled staff. After a few rather cryptic words, Nixon left matters to Bob Haldeman 'who was glaring sternly' and withdrew rapidly. Haldeman's message was disconcertingly blunt: 'I will expect resignations', he said, 'from every member of the staff, to be delivered to the staff secretary by noon on Friday, from each of you and each person who works for you. Also submit memos stating your preferences for new assignments.' He cleared his throat, paused and added, 'That is, of course, the courtesy customarily extended to a President at the start of each new administration.'

He then passed out envelopes filled with detailed instructions and forms. In his memoirs Nixon admits that this seemingly ungrateful attitude towards his faithful acolytes was a serious error on his own part.

Meanwhile, peace negotiations over Vietnam hung fire. Haig was despatched to Saigon on 9 November. President Thieu was still very obstinate, though Haig felt sure that he would 'come along in the end'. Kissinger dashed backwards and forwards, sometimes more optimistic than the facts warranted. On 13 December, Le Duc Tho, the chief North Vietnamese delegate, made it clear that he had no intention of reaching an agreement. At last Nixon was satisfied that nothing except force would improve the situation. On 14 December he issued an order to become effective three days thence, for the 'reseeding' of the mines in Haiphong Harbour, for resumed aerial reconnaissance and for B-52 strikes against military targets in the Hanoi–Haiphong complex. Of this order to renew bombing a week before Christmas he writes today, 'It was the most difficult decision I made during the entire war; at the same time, however, it was one of the most clear-cut and necessary ones.' The outcry was predictably passionate.

On 24 December he ordered a twenty-four-hour Christmas truce. But for 26 December he ordered one of the biggest bombing raids. That afternoon, however, the North Vietnamese sent the first signal that they had had enough. Talks were restarted. On 11 January Kissinger reported that an agreement had been reached. Thieu still remained obdurate, but Nixon told him that he would go ahead without him in the last resort. On 20 January Nixon was sworn in for his second term as the thirty-seventh President of the United States. On 23 January the Vietnam settlement was announced. On 27 January the cease-fire went into effect.

Goldwater's comments on the settlement must be taken seriously. 'When', he says, 'the United States policy makers decided to take advantage of our superior military capabilities, they brought the war to an end in approximately twelve days. It might have taken twelve weeks had we waged an all-out air and naval offensive earlier. It wouldn't have taken twelve years.' A reasonable point of view, but would it have been politically possible to give effect to it earlier?

Once again, however, Nixon did not feel the sense of relief

and satisfaction expected. He felt a surprising sense of sadness, apprehension and impatience: sadness, because Lyndon Johnson who died on 22 January had not lived a few extra days to share the moment with him and receive the tribute Nixon would have paid him; apprehension, because he had no illusions about the fragile nature of the agreement or about the communists' true motives in signing it; and impatience, because he was acutely aware of all the things they had postponed as a result of the war. But with his rational mind he was satisfied that he had achieved his objectives: first, the return of the American prisoners-of-war; second, a sporting chance for South Vietnam to maintain its independance.

About midnight he rang Kissinger, who could visualize Nixon brooding alone and himself indulged in some memorable reflections:

What extraordinary vehicles destiny selects to accomplish its design. This man, so lonely in his hour of triumph, so ungenerous in some of his motivations, had navigated our nation through one of the most anguishing periods in its history. Not by nature courageous, he had steeled himself to conspicuous acts of rare courage. Not normally outgoing, he had forced himself to rally his people to its challenge. He had striven for a revolution in American foreign policy so that it would overcome the disastrous oscillations between over-commitment and isolation. Despised by the Establishment, ambiguous in his human perceptions, he had yet held fast to a sense of national honour and responsibility, determined to prove that the strongest free country had no right to abdicate. ... He saw before him a vista of promise to which few statesmen have been blessed to aspire ... with all his insecurities and flaws he had brought us by a tremendous act of will to an extraordinary moment when dreams and possibilities conjoined.

10
Light on Darkness
January–April 1973

Meanwhile, a good deal had begun to happen in the unpleasant area of Watergate. Chuck Colson told me in 1978 that Nixon's absorption with peace in Vietnam precluded his giving any careful attention to the problem of Watergate in the six weeks following the election. In Colson's view this was when the last real chance existed of disposing of it effectively and honourably.

Nixon now recognizes that in the last weeks of December and the beginning of January the ground began to shift, however subtly. The Watergate trial was about to start and the pressure was mounting on the defendants. On 8 December Howard Hunt's wife had been killed in a plane crash. He blamed himself to the verge of total breakdown. He was now about to face a jail term. Colson became acutely worried about him. 'It now seems clear', writes Nixon, 'that I knew Colson was sending messages of reassurance to Hunt through his lawyer – messages that Hunt took to be signals of eventual clemency. I did not believe that any commitments had been made. I cannot even rule out the possibility that I knew similar reassurances were being given the other defendants. I certainly do not remember it, but where Watergate is concerned I have learned not to be categorical.' Vietnam, it cannot be repeated too often, dominated his thoughts at this time. When he dealt with Watergate in his diary, he recorded the opinion that Dean had acted like a smart political lawyer handling a volatile political case. The fact that he himself was, or might be, condoning crime did not seem to occur to the President. He kept repeating to himself and others that there was still no evidence that anyone in the White House had been involved in the break-in.

The law of obstruction of justice, it would seem (from Nixon's memoirs), was not present to his mind in this period or not until Dean drew his attention to it on 21 March. What, however, does seem rather extraordinary now is that Nixon should still be able to write, with no apparent sense of contradiction: 'As certain as I was that we had done everything to contain the Watergate scandal, I was equally as confident that we had not tried to cover it up. For one thing there was no question that the FBI's investigation had been extensive.' In retrospect it is clear that Nixon was playing two parts at once. On the one hand he was trying to look after the interests of his own side and his own staff in the same way as anybody not concerned with law enforcement would think it his duty. On the other hand he was persuading himself that he was giving the forces of law and order their proper encouragement to expose the guilty. Perhaps American Presidents were so accustomed to wearing two or more hats that the contradiction did not and still does not strike him.

By February things were looking worse. 'I was still concerned about the widespread impression of a cover-up that had set in, yet there was little we could do.' He still persuaded himself that he was not covering up anything. He said to Colson: 'We are not covering up a damn thing.' Colson emphatically agreed. By that he meant that they were allowing the forces of law and order and prosecution to go ahead unimpeded.

So runs Nixon's account. Colson tells the story more graphically. He describes his last meeting with the President as his special counsel before his return to the law. He had just come back from a visit to Moscow as Nixon's emissary. The trip was discussed, then Colson brought up the subject of Watergate: 'Whoever did order Watergate, let it out!' he said emotionally. 'Let's get rid of it now, take our losses.' He had barely got the words out before the President dropped his feet from his mahogany desk on to the floor and came straight up in his chair. '"Who do you think did this? Mitchell? Magruder?" He was staring intently into my eyes, face flushed, anger in his voice. I had struck a raw nerve, but I was convinced at that moment that he was as much in the dark as I was.'

On 14 February Nixon met Pat Gray, acting Director of the FBI, whom Nixon wished to nominate as permanent Director. Gray was sure that he could convince even non-believers that the FBI had proceeded without showing favour in the Watergate investigation. Nixon in his diary in mid-February is still recording: 'Gray can tell a pretty good story. It is a true story of a thorough investigation and this of course knocks down the cover-up.' But suddenly it was the end of February. The Ervin hearings [the Senate inquiry] were breathing down their necks. The critical issue had still not been decided of whether they would invoke executive privilege and refuse to let any White House aides testify. The Republicans in Congress were getting anxious; the problem was beginning to snowball.' Nixon decided to work directly with John Dean, a fatal decision as it proved, and 'to give the matter his personal attention'.

On 27 and 28 February he had talks with Dean which seem rather pathetic, looking back. 'I am', he wrote, 'very impressed by him. He has shown enormous strength, great intelligence and great subtlety.' The truth is that Nixon was completely taken in by Dean. Not that Dean was deliberately working against him at that time, but, in his early thirties, he had simply not got the experience or character to be entrusted with so important a role. Nixon was clearly delighted with what he calls 'an amazing recitation as to how Johnson had used the FBI', and how earlier the Truman administration 'had put up a stone wall when we tried to conduct an investigation'. All this clearly eased Nixon's conscience at the time; it was to prove of no value whatever when the issues were fought out in public.

At the end of February, the worst news was the disastrous confirmation hearings before the Senate of Gray as Director of the FBI. To quote Woodward and Bernstein, 'The reporters watched in amazement as day after day Gray attested to the ineptitude, if not the criminal negligence, of his supervision of the FBI's investigation. He volunteered the information that he had turned over the files of the investigation to John Dean.' Later, on 22 March, he testified that John Dean 'had probably lied when he told the FBI on 22 June that he did not know if Howard Hunt had an office in the White House'. The White House issued an unequivocal denial, but the damage was done.

Dean and Nixon continued to meet during the first weeks of March. On 13 March they were discussing the press conference which Nixon would be facing on 15 March. There was at least one unpleasant shock. Haldeman had given Chapin and Gordon Strachan, a Haldeman aide, the approval to start the 'Segretti' operation and the press was continually trying to link Segretti to Watergate. Dean reassured Nixon that Chapin had not known anything about Watergate. 'Did Strachan?' asked Nixon, almost perfunctorily. 'Yes,' replied Dean. Nixon was startled: 'He knew?' 'Yes.' 'About the Watergate?' 'Yes,' Dean repeated. Nixon was stunned – this was appalling. 'Well then,' he said, 'Bob knew.' But in the same breath he added, 'He may not have.' Nixon was partly reassured but only partly. 'I'll be damned,' he concluded. 'Well, that's the problem in Bob's case.... It's not Chapin then, but Strachan. Because Strachan worked for him [Haldeman].' This must be regarded as a crucial moment in Nixon's investigation of the truth about Watergate. 'I still had difficulty accepting the fact that, according to Dean, Strachan had known about the Watergate bugging. If this was true, then nine months of denial of White House involvement were undermined.' In other words, it would seem that a dishonest defence had been presented to the world though, in Nixon's case, it had been honest enough.

By this time Nixon was on the eve of what he fairly called a partisan Senate inquisition, 'suddenly facing serious and undefined vulnerabilities'. Dean warned him that it would be highly dangerous to allow the White House staff to 'go up and testify'. The press conference of 15 March began straight away to concentrate on Watergate and on Dean's role. Nixon by now faced with the media and Congress realized for the first time the dimensions of the problem regarding Watergate: 'Vietnam had found its successor.' He also knew immediately that his current approach to Watergate was not going to work: 'We already looked as if we had something to hide.' He still clung, precariously now, to the fact that no one in the White House had been involved in the Watergate break-in. Dean had modified his original assertion that Strachan had known in advance to one that he had known after the event.

Nixon was still pinning his hopes, futile though they seemed to be, on a written statement from Dean repeating that there was no evidence against Colson, Chapin or Haldeman on Watergate. But unwelcome pieces of information did not stop coming in. Dean revealed that he himself had been present at meetings in John Mitchell's office at which Gordon Liddy's intelligence-gathering plans had been discussed. 'But you didn't hear any discussion of bugging, did you?' asked Nixon. 'Or did you?' 'Yeah, I did,' answered Dean.

Nixon was now beginning to slide away from a policy of candour. He told Dean that he had better not mention the talk about bugging in the statement he was going to prepare. He rationalized that after all Dean had tried to stop it and Mitchell had not approved it while Dean was present. Things were getting more complicated every day.

Dean's revelations were not over. Now it was Ehrlichman who was in danger. He had a problem with both Hunt and Liddy, not in connection with Watergate but previously. In 1971 Dean told Nixon that Hunt and Liddy, laden with CIA equipment, had broken into the office of Daniel Ellsberg's psychiatrist. 'What in the world—?!' exclaimed Nixon. This was another bolt from the blue. Dean explained that they were trying to get some information on Ellsberg from his doctor about his psychiatric condition. The episode was going to prove disastrous enough, but for the time being Nixon consoled himself with the reflection that the Ellsberg case could not come up during the formal hearings.

Nixon turned his mind desperately to foreign policy. But he and Haldeman were by now equally frustrated about the absence of action on Watergate. It was 20 March and, in Nixon's words, 'We were back exactly where we had been four days after the break-in nine months earlier: no one was sure about Mitchell or – on a first-hand basis – even about Magruder....' But the circumstantial involvements and vulnerabilities surrounding Watergate were so great that even false allegations made by a Liddy or a Magruder could be fatal.

Haldeman brought up one other problem at the end of a meeting with Nixon on 20 March. Three hundred and fifty thousand dollars in cash had been transferred out of the campaign funds in 1972 and brought to the White House for such political projects as private polling. The money had not been used, and after the election had been transferred back to CRP. Haldeman feared that there might be more in this than he had yet discovered, and so it was to prove.

Before the end of the day Dean pressed Nixon for a meeting as soon as possible. He seemed slightly agitated; he wanted a fuller and more systematic discussion than they had yet had. Not for the first time when the idea of a statement arose Dean was 'cool'; he wanted first a personal meeting with Nixon. In his diary that evening, Nixon reported that one of the major concerns was what would happen when the judge passed sentences on the Watergate defendants. He was apparently going to be extremely tough, which did not surprise Nixon. Anxiety was mounting that McCord might crack and inform the Judge that he was ready to tell all. 'Certainly', wrote Nixon in his diary, 'he knows a hell of a lot about Mitchell. Mitchell is the one I am most concerned about,' and yet he could never bring himself to have it out with him. One comment of his about Mitchell is all too human: 'Mitchell just didn't keep his hand on the tiller at a time when he was having all the problems with Martha although I do not blame him for it. I know why it happened.'

21 March 1973 ranks with 23 June 1972 as a day which destroyed Nixon. Indeed, it ranks higher in retrospect. The White House tapes, including the tape of 23 June, could never have been extracted from the White House unless public opinion had overwhelmingly supported the demand for them. There is little doubt that it was Dean's evidence which swung public opinion against Nixon in the critical period. Nixon must therefore be held to have mishandled Dean seriously and turned one of his most confidential assistants into a remorseless enemy. He managed to achieve this after a day of discus-

sions which could be presented by Dean in a most damaging light when he turned enemy.

Yet when John Dean entered the Oval Office at ten o'clock on Wednesday morning, 21 March, he was probably still anxious to help the President. He certainly began by giving Nixon the bluntest of warnings. 'I think', he said, 'that there is no doubt about the seriousness of the problem.... We've got... we have a cancer within – close to the presidency that's growing. It's growing daily. It's compounding – it grows geometrically now because it compounds itself. One, we're being blackmailed; two, people are going to start perjuring themselves very quickly that have not had to perjure themselves to protect other people and the like. And there is no assurance....' 'That it won't bust,' Nixon supplied. 'That it won't bust,' Dean repeated.

Dean ran over the events leading to the break-in, with which we are now familiar. Then he turned to the post-break-in activities. He said that he himself had been under 'pretty clear instructions' not really to investigate this [the break-in?], and had acted on a theory of containment. Soon after the arrests at Watergate, the defendants had warned: 'We've got to have attorneys' fees, if you're asking us to take this through the election.' Arrangements were made for the payment at meetings where Dean and Mitchell were present. Kalmbach (Nixon's lawyer) was brought in. Kalmbach raised some cash. Dean delivered his punchline: 'Bob is involved in that. John is involved in that. Mitchell is involved in that. And that's an obstruction of justice.'

Nixon still thought Dean was over-dramatizing. Dean said that Haldeman had let him use a $350,000 cash fund (the fund mentioned by Haldeman the night before), which had been held at the White House to make payments to the defendants. He, Haldeman and Ehrlichman had decided that there was 'no price too high to pay not to let this thing blow up in front of the election'. Nixon's next remark seems to carry him a long way into the cover-up: 'I think you should handle that one pretty fast,' he said to Dean, who mentioned bluntly other problems. 'Colson had talked indirectly to Hunt about commutation.' But Dean had still to reach the worst part of his message. Hunt was demanding $122,000 for attorney's fees and personal expenses. Hunt's message had been accompanied by a threat: 'I will bring John Ehrlichman down to his knees and put him in jail. I have done enough seamy things for him and Krogh. He would never survive it.' Hunt's deadline, according to Dean, was close of business yesterday.

The next two sentences in Nixon's memoirs summarize his appalling dilemma by this time. 'Hunt's threat was just the most urgent and dramatic example of the larger problem of the continuing blackmail possibilities for all the defendants. If we continued to pay it, that would compound the obstruction of justice.' And if they didn't, ruin stared at them, not because of the original break-in, but because of the obstruction of justice, as a court might well look on it since that time. There was also the question of how to raise the money without involving the White House. Dean estimated that payments for the defendants would require a million dollars over the next few years. Nixon said that it would not be easy, but he knew where the money could be obtained. (He had in mind previous large contributors.) The discussion went on and on. One thing was clear. Howard Hunt was a time-bomb and his dead-line was 'yesterday'. In two days he would be sentenced and he would be sure to make good on his threat. What was Nixon ready to consider? What did he actually agree to in his conversations with Dean, with Haldeman later present? The subject has been combed backwards and forwards by friends and enemies, particularly enemies in the light of Dean's evidence later in the year and, more conclusively, tapes which were produced in 1974.

Nixon summarizes the discussion and no one seems to be able to controvert this statement. 'Only two decisions had emerged. Haldeman was to have Mitchell come down from New York immediately for a talk with Dean and Ehrlichman, and Dean was to try to get the sentencing postponed.' No agreement was reached to make payment to anyone. (Any payment actually made to defendants had been decided on already, without Nixon's knowledge.)

Meanwhile, however, Nixon had used various expressions which were to tell heavily against him later on. 'Just looking at the immediate problem', he had said, 'don't you have to handle Hunt's financial situation damn soon? You've got to keep the cap on the bottle that much, in order to have any options. Either that or let it blow right now' – and there were other sayings in line with that approach. He came back near the end to the problem of Hunt: 'We agreed that no more payments should be made to all the defendants, but Hunt was still the time-bomb. I told Haldeman the reason the Hunt problem worried me was that it had nothing to do with the campaign, it had to do with the Ellsberg thing.'

But there was no easy way out in practice, whatever the ethics. In Nixon's words, 'the extreme measure of paying blackmail was not the solution. It would only buy a little time.'

Those familiar with Nixon's habits of discussion will refuse to accept some of the hypotheses he was ready to consider as committing him morally. He said other things which showed that his sense of propriety had not evaporated. Dean had said, in regard to a promise of clemency, even after the 1974 elections, 'It may further involve you in a way you shouldn't be involved.' 'No, it's wrong, that's for sure,' said Nixon. Later, Dean said earnestly, 'We cannot let you be tarnished,' and Nixon heartily agreed with him: 'I say that the White House can't do it. Right?' And the meeting ended. No fair-minded person could say that Nixon had *agreed* to any further payments to Hunt, nor on the other hand deny that he had been ready and was still ready to consider them.

Intimate advisers of Nixon, Colson for example, recall his penchant for playing devil's advocate in a discussion, in order to make sure that no angle, however unwelcome, was ignored. Heard on tape, some of the topics raised in this way might seem like courses of action he had actually favoured.

Nothing constructive had really emerged, except the idea of those concerned going before a grand jury. Looking back, that seems a fairly useless proposal. Nixon's diary comments on 21 March are rather extraordinary. In his memoirs, he describes it as a day that was later to be seen as a disastrous turning-point in his presidency. In the diary he remarks: 'As far as the day was concerned it was relatively uneventful, except for the talk with Dean ... he is obviously very depressed and doesn't really see anything – other course of action open, but to move to let the facts out.'

Nixon left the meeting quite unaware, as he now realizes,

that Dean was trying to alert him to the fact that the question of who had authorized the break-in was now subsidiary to the far more serious problem of the cover-up. Even Dean's insistence that the authorization of payments to the defendants was an obstruction of justice seemed to Nixon to be more of a reflection of Dean's personal depression than a statement of a considered legal conclusion. He left the 21 March meeting more disturbed than shocked, more anxious than alarmed. Only three weeks later, he tells us, when he finally saw the whole cover-up mosaic in perspective and realized the part that the payments to the defendants played in it, would he understand what Dean had really been trying to tell him.

On 23 March Judge Sirica announced some sensational sentences. He gave a provisional sentence of thirty-five years to Hunt and forty to each of the others. Liddy was given 'six years and eight months to twenty years' and a $40,000 fine.

A high American legal authority, not friendly to Nixon, had stated that there is no support in American constitutional practice for this 'judicial blackmail'. Ethical or not, the tactics of Sirica, the trial judge, were likely to prove all too effective for Nixon's welfare. The Nixon camp continued to conduct their pathetically ineffective discussions.

The arguments still went on as to whether or not to go before the grand jury. At one moment Nixon favoured it, but later, when Dean revived it, he seemed reluctant. It was 'at this period [23 March] that Dean telephoned from Camp David. He told Haldeman's assistant, Higby, that "while Dean's report might not be a good defence as far as the rest of the White House staff was concerned, it was a very good defence of John Dean".' Dean by this time seemed to be setting out to carve a defence for himself on the assumption that some of the others would inevitably be for the high jump.

In early April, Dean told Haldeman that he was going to have an off-the-record meeting with US attorneys the next day. He said that there was no interest in post-break-in activities. Nixon made a note about the unfortunate way the whole situation was developing. But he still expressed optimism about his ability to survive it: 'Every one is going into business for himself, but we are not going to let it get to the point that one destroys another.' Vain hope indeed!

In early April, Ehrlichman told Nixon that in legal terms motive would be the key to guilt or innocence in the authorization of these payments. If the purpose had been to provide attorneys' fees and family support, then they were legal. If the purpose had been to buy silence from the defendants, that would be an obstruction of justice.

Nixon argues that the purpose of course was to see that defendants would get adequate counsel and that their families would be taken care of during the period when they were in jail. Hunt was bitterly critical of the White House for not being generous enough in this respect. Nixon, however, admits in his diary, 'But I suppose it could be said that they were being paid to shut up and not talk. Now whether or not this is a crime remains to be seen.'

'When it came', he continues, 'to questions of motive, the real answer lay in each man's mind and each man's conscience.' His conclusion was that everyone involved should get together and stick to the line that they did not raise the money to obstruct justice. In his own words a few days later: 'I don't mean a lie, but a line.' Whatever the precise legalities, it must surely seem reasonable that money should be raised for the legal expenses and family support of the dependants. On the other hand, those close to the President and the President himself had a strong interest in conciliating Hunt and the others.

By 13 April 'it seemed as if their return to Washington had somehow been a catalyst. Charges and counter-charges were now flying in every direction.... A panic was setting in that was beyond everyone's control. Everyone was accusing everyone else or saying that they were vulnerable. Soon we could no longer avoid facing the unpleasant fact that the whole thing was completely out of hand and that something had to be done to get the White House "out in front".' Now it was not just a question of knowledge of the Watergate break-in or subsequent cover-up; he might well have to respond to accusations that he had not acted promptly on the knowledge obtained during the last few weeks.

Nixon in restrospect makes no attempt to hide the extraordinary feebleness of the discussions in the three weeks following Dean's statement to him (21 March) that there was a cancer close to the presidency. Every alternative course of action met with objections from one or other of his aides or friends who suddenly found himself in a vulnerable position. As a result, in the three weeks after 21 March, when Dean in his own words 'had officially put me on notice about the implications of cover-up, we did nothing more than stew and worry about the shifting facts and continued to look for any way to prevent damage'. Yet he himself admits that during these three weeks Watergate 'had been my almost constant preoccupation'. How was it that this man, so enormously effective almost always, was so utterly futile in a matter that concerned his whole political survival, to which he was giving the fullest possible attention?

Nixon refers to 14 April as 'the day when everything began to fall apart'. Magruder had begun to 'talk to' the US attorneys. 'The loose cannon had finally gone off.' Even now, halfway through April, Nixon still did not realize his full peril. He was genuinely sorry for his dedicated assistants who had gone too far through excessive zeal and were likely to be ruined. Realistic as ever, he notes with qualified satisfaction the fact that the latest Gallup poll indicated approval/disapproval at 60/33. Only 5 per cent were as yet, so it seemed, affected by Watergate, but he faces the likelihood, in his diary for that date, that the verdict would not be as favourable 'for some time'. Even this limited optimism was on the point of ending. He remarks, poignantly enough, 'This, April 14, was to be my last full diary dictation until June 1974. Events became so cheerless that I no longer had the time or the desire to dictate reflections.'

15 April was another critical day, a turning-point in the sad story of Watergate, though not because of any particular decisions. Attorney-General Kleindienst came to the President's office and told him that Haldeman and Ehrlichman were 'being drawn into the criminal case on Watergate'. He said that the main accuser was John Dean. Dean had in fact acknowledged his own role in obstructing justice and was now involving others.

He said he thought that the President should consider whether Haldeman and Ehrlichman should take leave of absence now in anticipation of what might come.

Kleindienst was highly emotional and his voice choked periodically. He had been up nearly the whole night and his eyes were red with fatigue and tears. He described the charges: Dean had alleged that shortly after the break-in Ehrlichman had told him to 'deep-six' materials from Hunt's safe and to get Hunt out of the country; Haldeman was accused of knowing that the $350,000 he sent back to the CRP was used to pay the defendants; and there was a question whether Haldeman had actually seen budget proposals from Magruder that outlined the bugging plans.

The charges based on Dean's accusations did not seem to Nixon to be sufficient evidence to indict either Haldeman or Ehrlichman. But Kleindienst returned later with Peterson, the Assistant Attorney-General. Peterson told Nixon that he thought Haldeman and Ehrlichman should resign. 'I can't fire men', said Nixon, 'simply because of the appearance of guilt. I have to have *proof* of their guilt.' 'What you have just said, Mr President, speaks very well of you as a man,' said Peterson; 'it does not speak well of you as a President.' Next day Nixon broke the news to Haldeman and Ehrlichman that both Kleindienst and Peterson felt they should leave the White House. 'They were stunned, as I had been.' Dean sent word that the motivation for his actions was loyalty. (He was being offered the good offices of the US Attorney-General in return for his co-operation.) When he saw Nixon he said that, regardless of what their motives might have been, Haldeman and Ehrlichman were involved in an obstruction of justice, 'which is as broad as the imagination of man'.

Dean seemed almost cocky about his own position; he seemed confident that his lawyers would succeed in plea-bargaining with the prosecutors. He obviously expected to get immunity; he expected also that Haldeman and Ehrlichman would be convicted.

That same day, 15 April, Nixon saw Haldeman and Ehrlichman again and told them about Dean's verdict of conspiracy by circumstance. They urged that Dean should be dismissed. But Peterson was insistent that Dean should not be forced to leave the White House, lest such a move adversely affect his decision to co-operate.

When Nixon saw Dean on Monday 16 April he gave him two draft letters, one tendering his resignation, the other requesting leave of absence. But Dean by now was tense and much less self-assured. He seemed determined to prove that Haldeman and Ehrlichman were as guilty as he was, indeed more so. Later it would occur to Nixon that what he really wanted was immunity for himself. But this, wisely or otherwise, Nixon would not provide for him. In a public statement on 17 April he announced: 'I have expressed to the appropriate authorities my view that no individual holding in the past or at the present a position of major importance in the administration should be given immunity from prosecution.'

When Dean heard of this statement, he went 'charging round the White House like a wild animal'. Two days later, the *Washington Post* reported that Jeb Magruder was telling everything to the prosecutor and that his story would bring down John Dean. The story said that he accused Mitchell and Dean of helping plan the break-in. This, in Nixon's word, 'triggered' Dean to go all-out in the exposure of his employer and colleagues.

For the next fortnight, the crucial question was whether Nixon should or should not get rid of Haldeman and Ehrlichman. He came round to the conclusion that they would have to go. The circumstantial facts were so damning that they would not be able to survive the political scrutiny. Nixon told himself that he had not been involved in the things that gave them potential criminal vulnerability. He was sure that he had heard nothing about the break-in in advance; he had seen none of the reports based on the phone bug; he had known nothing about Ehrlichman's alleged instruction to Dean to 'deep-six' the material from Hunt's safe; and he was sure that no one had asked him about bringing in Kalmbach to raise funds, or about using the \$350,000 cash fund for the payments to the defendants.

But there were things he had known. He had talked with Colson about clemency; he too had suspected that Magruder was not telling the truth, but he had done nothing about his suspicions; he had been aware that support funds were going to the defendants; and on 21 March he had even contemplated paying blackmail. The difference was that Haldeman and Ehrlichman had become trapped by their circumstantial involvement; so far, in his own eyes, he had not.

Nixon was faced with having to fire his friends for things he himself was a part of, things that he could not accept as morally or legally wrong, no matter how much that opened him to charges of cynicism and amorality. 'I was selfish enough', he writes, 'about my own survival to want them to leave; but I was not so ruthless as to be able to confront easily the idea of hurting people I cared about so deeply. I worried about the impact on them if they were forced to leave; and I worried about the impact on me if they didn't.' So the next two weeks were governed by contradictory impulses. He tried to persuade them to go – while he insisted that he could not offer up his friends as sacrifices. He said that they had to do the right thing, no matter how painful it was – while he cast about for any possible way to avert the damage, even 'if it took us to the edge of the law'.

Nixon was meanwhile avoiding another decision in regard to Dean. He had already begun to alienate him by not agreeing to grant him immunity. 'Now I knew that if I seemed to turn on him, he would almost certainly turn on me.' He wanted to handle Dean 'very gingerly'. In the result he got the worst of all worlds. Dean more than any other individual was to prove his downfall.

Meanwhile, the dangers to Haldeman and Ehrlichman increased hour by hour. On 19 April the papers began to come out with stories of the exposures which Dean would shortly be making. On Easter morning there were four different Watergate stories on the front page of the *Washington Post*, favourable to Dean and unfavourable to Haldeman and Ehrlichman. That morning Nixon, following his regular custom, rang up Colson, Haldeman, Ehrlichman and Dean. His message to the last of these reads incredibly now: 'On Easter morning I want you to know some one is thinking about you. I want to wish you well – we'll make it through. You said that this is a cancer that must be cut out. I want you to know that I am following that advice.' He added that Dean was still his counsel. Yet by this time he must have known that Dean was starting to betray him.

On Monday morning, 23 April, Nixon had a three-hour session with Ziegler, his Press Secretary, Pat Buchanan, his speech-writer, and Chappie Rose, 'a fine lawyer and personal friend'. As the session drew to an emotional end, all agreed that Haldeman and Ehrlichman had to resign. Nixon further sought the advice of others, several men he particularly trusted and respected. The general verdict was that Haldeman and Ehrlichman must go.

In the last two weeks of April, Nixon at last began facing the likelihood that he would be Dean's next target and that he had personally supplied him with the ammunition during the 21 March conversation. 'When I was honest with myself I had to admit that I had genuinely contemplated paying blackmail to Hunt – not because of Watergate, but because of his threat against Ehrlichman on the break-in at Ellsberg's psychiatrist's office and against the administration in general.' He had also talked with Dean about the possibility of continuing payments to the other defendants. Furthermore, in that conversation Dean had made him aware of payments to defendants that, in Dean's view, constituted an obstruction of justice.

Nixon became more and more disturbed at the thought that Dean might have carried a tape-recorder at the meeting on 21 March. On 25 April, Haldeman came to report on his first couple of hours' listening to the tape of the 21 March conversation. His report was rather more encouraging than it might have been. It was clear that no action had been taken as a result of the conversation. Nixon had not finally ordered any payments to be made to the defendants and he had ruled out clemency. He told Haldeman that he had always wondered about the taping equipment, 'but I'm damned glad we have it, aren't you?' 'Yes, Sir,' Haldeman answered, adding that the one section he had been through had been helpful.

By 26 April, Dean's attempt to plea-bargain with the prosecutors had broken down. He was sending threatening new signals to the White House. There was a story that Pat Gray, Director of the FBI, had burned evidence from Hunt's safe. Gray, it was said, was going to accuse Ehrlichman and Dean of instructing him to destroy the papers.

Soon the *New York Times* was ringing the White House with the news that Dean was implicating the President. On the *Washington Post* Bernstein did not know what to think. Of all the Watergate principals he probably had the least regard for John Dean. 'John Mitchell was his own man. Colson's intellect was first rate. Somebody to respect at the poker table regardless of what you thought of him. Haldeman was an enigma. Sometimes brilliant, often pitifully short-sighted, often cruel, sometimes appealingly human.' But 'Dean had not seemed to have any substance'. A WASP, Sammy Glick, who had not even been very imaginative about the way he climbed to the top, but 'he must know a lot'. They could not afford to neglect him as a source of information. By this time, they and other journalists were relentlessly milking the associates of the principal characters, each of whom could be relied upon to tell a tale favourable to their own friend and unfavourable to his colleagues.

Lawyers acting for Haldeman and Ehrlichman insisted to the President that their clients were being taken advantage of because they were loyal and Dean was not. But Dean's associate was telling the reporters that the President had been 'persuaded by the German shepherds (Haldeman and Ehrlichman) to keep his losses to a minimum ... to sacrifice John Dean while trying to discourage the indictment of Haldeman and Ehrlichman. The P. is ready to give John the final shove.' Inevitably it was now beginning to be each man for himself, though Haldeman was still inflexibly loyal.

On Friday night, 27 April, Nixon flew to Camp David. In the morning of 28 April he found Tricia sitting in the living-room. She had been talking all night with Julie and her husband David, and for a long time with Pat in the morning. They were all agreed that he had no choice but to have Haldeman and Ehrlichman resign. 'You know I never felt that the way they handled people served you well.' Her eyes brimmed with tears as she added: 'Whatever you do, just remember we will support you, and we love you very much.'

That evening Ehrlichman rang Nixon. He told him that he thought that Nixon should recognize the reality of his own responsibility. All the illegal acts ultimately derived from him, whether directly or indirectly. He implied, so Nixon thought, that the President should resign.

Early on Sunday morning Nixon called Haldeman and asked if he would come to Camp David. He said he would and so would Ehrlichman. But they would like to have separate meetings with Nixon. Nixon knew that Haldeman realized that the end had come.

Haldeman arrived in the early afternoon of Sunday 29 April. Nixon told him that resignation was the right course for him and that this was the hardest decision he had ever made. 'I told him that when I went to bed last night, I had hoped and almost prayed that I wouldn't wake up this morning.' Nixon admitted that this wasn't fair, but he saw no other way. 'I told him that I felt enormous guilt. I knew that the responsibility and much of the blame for what had happened rested with me.' Haldeman responded in stoical, almost heroic fashion. Even at this moment his effort was to reassure Nixon, who must always feel he could call on him. He accepted the decision, even though he did not agree with it. 'You have to remember', he said, 'that nothing that has happened in the Watergate mess has changed your mandate in the non-Watergate area. That is what matters, that is what you do best.'

Haldeman left, walked out into the porch and stood there, looking down into the valley. Ehrlichman arrived. Nixon shook hands and said, 'I know what a terribly difficult day this is for you. I am sure you realize what a difficult day it is for me.' Nixon told him also about his feelings the night before and his hope that he would not wake up in the morning. Ehrlichman put his arm around his shoulders and said: 'Don't talk that way; don't think that way.'

Nixon expressed his wish to help him with the heavy financial burdens, including attorneys' fees, now likely to fall on him. Ehrlichman's mouth tightened and he said quickly: 'There is only one thing I would like for you to do. I would like for you to explain this to my children.' With controlled bitterness, Ehrlichman said that the decision Nixon had made was wrong and that he would live to regret it. 'I have no choice but to accept it, and I will,' he said. 'But I still feel I have done nothing that was without your implied or direct approval.' 'You have always been the conscience of the administration,' said Nixon. 'You were always for the cleanest way through things.' 'If I was the conscience then I haven't been very effective,' Ehrlichman replied.

The holocaust was not yet completed. Later the same afternoon Kleindienst, still Attorney-General, came to see Nixon. His close association with Mitchell now made it impossible for him to stay on. Nixon and he agreed that he should resign, though this was a decision he was in no way proud of. 'I deeply regret now,' adds Nixon in his memoirs, 'that Kleindienst's departure was timed to coincide with the others. It falsely conveyed the impression that he was somehow involved in Watergate.' So now he had lost, or was about to lose, them all: Mitchell, Colson, Haldeman, Ehrlichman, Dean and Kleindienst. It is almost incredible, looking back, that he could have hoped to survive himself. But we must never forget that he still possessed an enormous sense of a mission to be performed and that between now and August 1974 he went a long way to perform it.

Nixon accepted the letters of resignation of Haldeman and Ehrlichman. They walked out to the car together. They said bolstering things like: 'Get up for your speech tomorrow night.' 'I wish I were as strong as you,' said Nixon. 'God bless you both.' The car drove away. Nixon was under no illusions about the damage he had done them. These men had been his closest aides, they were his friends. He tried to make it up to them the next night by saying in his speech what he deeply believed. 'Today, in one of the most difficult decisions of my presidency, I accepted the resignations of two of my closest associates in the White House – Bob Haldeman, John Ehrlichman – two of the finest public servants it has been my privilege to know.' But he was well aware that, by asking them to leave, he had ensured that they would never be able to prove that their motives had been innocent. 'I had done what I felt was necessary, but not what I believed was right' – a curious distinction; another way, perhaps, of saying that the end justifies the means.

Nixon had always prided himself on the fact that he stood by people who were down, but, 'Now I had sacrificed for myself two people to whom I owed so much.' That is how he accuses himself in retrospect. But which of us is to say that he made the wrong decision in accepting these resignations, if to quit was the only alternative?

This speech (on the Monday) was an agonizing exercise. He handed a draft of it to Ray Price, saying, 'You are the most honest, cool, objective man I know. If you feel that I should resign, I am ready to do so. You won't have to tell me. You should just put it in the next draft.' Price told him that he should not resign, that he had a duty to complete the job he had been elected to perform. But no one can question the pain felt by Nixon then and later. 'I felt as if I had cut off one arm and then the other.' The amputation may have been necessary for even a chance of survival. 'But what I had had to do left me so anguished and saddened that from that day on the presidency lost all joys for me.'

The speech (30 April 1973) was the first time he had formally addressed the American people specifically on Watergate. They were waiting for a 'yes' or 'no' answer to the question of whether he also was involved. 'I believe', he writes, 'that a totally honest answer would have been neither a simple "yes" or "no".' If he had given the true answer, he would have had to say that, without fully realizing the implications of his actions, he had become deeply entangled in the complicated mesh of decisions, inactions, misunderstandings and conflicting motivations that comprised the Watergate cover-up; he would have had to admit that he still did not know the whole story and therefore did not know the full extent of his own involvement in it; and he would have had to give the damaging specifics of what he did know, while leaving open the possibility that much more might come out later.

But he was much too experienced a politician to suppose that such a complicated explanation at that date would have been tolerated. In no way would it have enabled him to survive politically. 'I decided', he writes 'to answer "no" to the question whether I was also involved in Watergate.' He hoped that by a bold assertion of innocence he would once and for all be able to put Watergate behind him as a nagging national issue. 'I could not', he writes, 'have made a more disastrous miscalculation.'

He frankly spells out the degree to which his speech of 30 April was less than truthful. In that speech he gave the impression that he had known nothing at all about the cover-up until his 21 March meeting with Dean. He indicated that once he had learned about it he had acted with despatch and dispassion to end it. 'In fact,' he writes, 'I had known some of the details of the cover-up before 21 March, and when I did become aware of their implications, instead of exerting presidential leadership aimed at uncovering the cover-up, I embarked upon an increasingly desperate search for ways to limit the damage to my friends, my administration and to myself.'

The first and decisive stage of the cover-up was complete by 30 April 1973. From then on, Nixon would be advised by officials who were in no circumstances prepared to participate in further operations of doubtful legality. But he was still a slave of the immediate past, trying desperately to prevent the exposure of the preceding cover-up and driven, therefore, to conceal essential facts from the American public. In the sixteen months that followed, in spite of the appalling handicap of Watergate, Nixon accomplished much of permanent value in the international arena. We may or may not accept the case for his staying on as President but, if we do, we accept also the necessity for covering up the cover-up. He had otherwise no hope of survival.

For his serious critics, the nine months from the end of June 1972 to the end of April 1973 was the essential period. If he is to be condemned it is for what he did or failed to do regarding Watergate during that time (putting aside for the moment an earlier responsibility for the atmosphere which led to Watergate).

The essential point was of course that he was clearly warned for the first time on 21 March that his aides were involved in a criminal activity, an obstruction of justice. Haldeman was involved, so was Ehrlichman, so was Mitchell, so was Dean. So clearly was he, the President, unless he cut himself off from the alleged conspiracy. And until 30 April Nixon would be hard put to it to say that he had cut himself off. What is astonishing to the laymen and perhaps to lawyers is that it needed John Dean, aged thirty-one, to tell Nixon, aged sixty, a lawyer of great acuteness, though not a *criminal* lawyer, that obstruction of justice was here involved.

A few months later every Tom, Dick or Harry could express his views about obstruction of justice, but it seemed to need John Dean's study of his law books to unearth the relevant statute. Four years later David Frost, with legal assistance, and Nixon himself were still debating the precise meaning of this statute which seemed almost as strange to Nixon as it was to Frost, although it had been passed into law during the Nixon presidency.

Looking at it in moral rather than legal terms, however, from 21 March Nixon's dilemma took on a new dimension of horror. For some months, he was now informed, his closest associates had been breaking the criminal law. There was one escape route open to him, which was to sack them all forthwith. It is almost inconceivable that he could have done so on 22 March. By the time he did so, on 30 April, after a grave warning from the prosecuting authorities, he had allowed himself to become still more deeply compromised.

In his speech of 30 April, Nixon admitted that, without fully realizing the implications of his action, he had become deeply entangled in the activities that comprised the Watergate cover-up. But he would probably still claim that he did nothing open to serious criticism until 21 March. With his sharp lawyer's mind, he drew a clear distinction between his conduct before and after that date. It was between 21 March and 30 April that, as he admitted to David Frost, he started acting 'as a lawyer for the defence' of his associates. He was the man with the chief responsibility for seeing that the laws of the United States were enforced. 'And to the extent that I did not meet that responsibility, to the extent that within the law, and in some cases going right to the edge of the law in trying to advise Ehrlichman and Haldeman and all the rest as to how best to present their cases, because I thought they were legally innocent, I came to the edge. And under the circumstances, I would have to say that a reasonable person could call that a cover-up.' He still does not admit that he broke the law but does admit that he went 'to the edge'.

11
Nixon–Rearguard Action
May–December 1973

From this point – May 1973 – until August 1974, it was to be a long rearguard action and a losing one. By the summer the White House and the Nixon Campaign Organization were under investigation by the FBI, the Ervin Committee and four other congressional committees, the General Accounting Office, one House committee, grand juries in Los Angeles, New York, Florida and Texas, and the Miami District Attorney's Office. More than a dozen civil suits had been filed. It is tempting to read the whole story of these fifteen months in those terms. But throughout the period Nixon was an active and, abroad at least, constructive President in spite of the immense handicap under which he was labouring. There were summit meetings with Brezhnev in June 1973 and June 1974. In the autumn the relationship so established was of high significance in establishing a reasonable peace in the Middle East. Later on, in 1976, after Nixon had been totally discredited in America, he was invited to China as their honoured guest. These achievements could never have come about if he had capitulated immediately under the Watergate pressures.

We must refrain from treating it as obvious that from May 1973 he was bound to be impeached or resign. In retrospect, he considers that, once the existence of the tapes was known and he had decided not to destroy them, his presidency had little chance of surviving to the end of its term. But he points out at the same time that he did not believe this when he decided not to destroy the tapes and, at the same time, try to prevent their publication. We must not forget that even while the shadows darkened – and by any human calculation he was likely to be destroyed one way or the other – he still regarded is more dishonourable to 'quit', that is to say resign, than be hurled from power by impeachment. He had, after all, only a few months earlier achieved an almost record electoral victory. In the middle of April he still had a majority of 60/30 in the opinion polls. He felt – and, as I see it, rightly so – that he had an obligation to the American people to stay at his post until he was forcibly evicted. One can call this obstinacy, if one likes. It can also be described as courage of a high order.

In the period between the beginning of May and the traumatic events of mid-October, there were only three crucial happenings directly related to Watergate: (1) the appointment of Archibald Cox as Special Prosecutor in May; (2) the evidence of John Dean for several days from 25 June, totalling over sixty television hours; (3) the disclosure of the existence of the tapes on 12 July. But, in a wider perspective, the summit meeting with Brezhnev from 18 June onwards might rate higher than any of these. And one cannot ignore the forced resignation of Vice-President Agnew. Taking the last point first, on 1 August Richardson, now Attorney-General, sent Agnew a letter informing him that he was being investigated on allegations of conspiracy, extortion, bribery and tax fraud. It was alleged that Agnew, while Governor of Maryland, had taken money in return for granting State contracts and that he continued to receive money in return for these past favours while he was Vice-President. To cut a painful story short, Agnew eventually reached an agreement with the prosecutors. He pleaded guilty to tax offences only; he was put on probation and therefore spared a prison term. These events were, to say the least, not helpful to the embattled President, although he was in no way directly connected with the improprieties alleged.

It may be simplest to summarize here the conference with Brezhnev. Just before 11 am on Monday morning, 18 June, Brezhnev's car came up the curving driveway to the south portico of the White House. Nixon welcomed him with the words: 'The hopes of the world rest with us at this time...' Brezhnev responded warmly: 'I and my comrades who have come with me are prepared to work hard to ensure that the talks we will have with you will justify the hopes of our peoples and serve the interests of a peaceful future for all mankind.' Brezhnev's warmth towards Nixon continued throughout the visit. 'Life', he said later, 'has led us to the conclusion that we must build a new relationship between our countries.' He announced that he had already invited Nixon to return to Russia in 1974 and that Nixon had accepted the invitation. Nixon felt that by 1973 the US overall still held the stronger hand, but compared with Krushchev in 1959, who was speaking from a position of weakness, Brezhnev could laugh and clown and vary his stern moods with warmth, based of the confidence that comes from holding some excellent cards.

The meetings at Camp David included long sessions on SALT, European security and the mutual and balanced force reductions generally. The Soviets felt that a renunciation of the use of nuclear weapons would greatly undercut American usefulness to the Chinese in the event of a Sino-Soviet war. But in Nixon's view a treaty of the kind they wanted would have wreaked havoc among NATO allies in Europe and countries like Israel and Japan that depended on American nuclear protection against the threat of Soviet attack. A somewhat meaningless formula was worked out by Kissinger and accepted. Later they repaired to San Clemente. Brezhnev spoke about China with deep anxiety. He was desperately anxious that America did not enter into any military agreement with China. He seems to have received a rather cryptic answer from Nixon.

Perhaps the most emotional discussion was one which took place from 10.30 pm until 1.30 am in Nixon's home. Brezhnev did everything in his power to 'browbeat' (Nixon's word) Nixon into imposing on Israel a settlement based on Arab terms, but he made no headway. Nixon kept reiterating that the important thing was to get talks started between the Arab States and Israel. Nixon remains convinced that Brezhnev was aware of the slow but steady progress that America had been making in re-opening the lines of communication between Washington and the Arab capitals. Brezhnev by no means wanted America to play the chief part in a peaceful settlement.

Nixon is still confident that the firmness he showed in that long night's session reinforced the seriousness of the message he conveyed to the Soviets when he ordered a military alert four months later during the Yom Kippur War.

The ex-President does not claim that it was possible so soon after the 1972 SALT agreements to effect another major break-through in that field. But he was satisfied to pin down Brezhnev to a new agreement by the end of 1974 when the discussions would centre on reductions and not just limitations of nuclear agreements. There were various subsidiary agreements signed at Summit II. From Nixon's point of view, the most useful result was his increased understanding of Brezhnev. He had spent forty-two hours with him in 1972, and now thirty-five hours. He was also convinced that Brezhnev returned home with a far better understanding of America and the Americans than he had had previously. The relationship between the two statesmen seemed to have become as intimate as was conceivable.

On 25 June, the day Brezhnev left Washington, the House of Representatives agreed to a Senate Bill immediately cutting off funds for US bombing action in Cambodia. The effect of this bill in Nixon's view was to deny him the means to enforce the Vietnam peace agreement and was therefore a horrible blow. He vetoed the bill. Eventually, a compromise reached in August 1973 required congressional approval for the funding of US military action in any part of Indo-China and weakened the whole presidential policy significantly. Later Congress denied first to Nixon and then to Ford the means to enforce the agreement when the North Vietnamese were openly violating it. They then began cutting back on military aid for South Vietnam at a time when the Soviets were increasing their aid to North Vietnam. In 1975, when the North Vietnamese launched their all-out invasion of the South, they had an advantage in arms, and the threat of American action to enforce the agreement had been totally removed. Whether or not one can share to the full Nixon's pride in the 1973 peace agreement, there is no doubt that it was sabotaged by the actions of Congress just described.

'In a spasm of short-sightedness and spite', he writes in *The Real War* 'the United States threw away what it had gained at such enormous cost.' President Wilson might have been forgiven for writing in similar terms about the American Senate who repudiated his noble vision of the League of Nations. In each case one can find serious errors to point to in the presidential performance. In neither case was there anything wrong with the dream.

Back now to Watergate. When Nixon, amid vociferous criticism, brought about the resignations of Haldeman and Ehrlichman he accepted the resignation of Kleindienst, the Attorney-General, who felt that he had been too much involved with Mitchell to continue in office. He appointed as his Chief of Staff General Alexander Haig, a soldier unmistakably possessed of the military virtues but not devoid of the political arts, some acquired as assistant to Henry Kissinger. Amid all the turmoil and tragedy ahead, he was to prove impeccably loyal to Nixon and to the American constitution alike. As Attorney-General Nixon chose Elliot Richardson, previously the Defence Secretary. One can understand why he selected this much-admired Boston Brahmin, but it was one of the most fatal steps he took throughout this period. Nixon had made the mistake in his speech of 30 April of giving him *carte blanche* in a wide and indeterminate area. In so doing he placed his political life in Richardson's hands.

Colson still considers that Richardson would have 'worked with the team' if Nixon had handled him more trustfully. As it was, Richardson not only appointed a Harvard lawyer called Archibald Cox as Special Prosecutor, but also gave him incredibly wide terms of reference which enabled him and his successor to investigate every aspect of Nixon's life including his tax returns. Nixon says today, and no doubt felt at the time, that there was no one in the whole of America whom he would have welcomed less as Special Prosecutor. Cox was a particular friend of the Kennedys and was soon drafting into his office all sorts of young Democratic lawyers with an immense animosity against Nixon. It must be said, in fairness, that Cox had a lofty reputation as a lawyer and that Richardson looked in vain elsewhere before having recourse to him.

But before Cox could get under way, Dean appeared before the Ervin Committee and testified at enormous length. Nixon in his memoirs points out many respects in which Dean's testimony was simply untrue. But there is no doubt (Nixon does not deny it) that Dean's evidence, relayed all over America on television, made a profound and indelible impression. Nixon describes his testimony on Watergate as an artful blend of truth and untruth, of possibly sincere misunderstandings and clearly conscious distortions. He convincingly rebuts most of Dean's charges about his (Nixon's) involvement in the cover-up from September to March, but he has this to say with creditable frankness: 'Dean's account of the crucial March 21 meeting was more accurate than my own had been.' Nixon's reputation with the general public never recovered from the evidence of one who had been so closely in his confidence and who betrayed that confidence with such an appalling air·of veracity.

Now came a shattering disclosure whose full effects would escalate as time went on. Nixon was stricken with a sharp, unpleasant attack of viral pneumonia. When he emerged from hospital on 12 July, it was to be greeted with the news that Haldeman's former aide, Alex Butterfield, had revealed the existence of the White House tape system to the Ervin Committee.

A word must be said here about the origin of the tapes. There had been an extensive taping system in the Johnson White House. Nixon, on coming into office, had ordered the entire system to be dismantled. But Johnson let him know that he considered it stupid to remove the system, which was the best way to preserve for history important White House transactions. The Nixon taping system was then installed very quickly. In his memoirs Nixon said that he was not comfortable with the idea of taping people without their knowledge, but he was at least confident that the secrecy of the system would protect their privacy.

Butterfield's excuse for this revelation has never been set out convincingly. Nixon was shocked by the news of it. To quote his own words: 'Impossible as it must seem now, I believed that the existence of the White House tape system would never be revealed.' It is certainly difficult to believe that at the present time. The question arose urgently as to whether the tapes should be destroyed. The first question that David Frost, in his television interviews, put to Nixon was: 'Why didn't you destroy the tapes?' Nixon made a note on 19 July when he first heard about the disclosure: 'Should have destroyed the tapes after April 30,' and one supposes that that is still his opinion.

Once the news of the tapes became public knowledge, it was obviously going to be very much harder. In his memoirs Nixon goes into the question at length of why he did not destroy them. The arguments for not doing so boil down to two: (1) That he thought that they were a mixed bag as far as he was concerned. This turned out completely wrong; (2) He was persuaded by Haig that destruction of the tapes would create an indelible impression of guilt. The attempt to invoke executive privilege to keep them from being made public appeared hardly less guilty than destroying them, and in fact he was gradually forced to bring them into the light of day.

October 1973 was a memorable month in the life story of Richard Nixon. On the highest plane of international statesmanship, it saw him at the peak of his powers. But the tin can of Watergate tied to his tail rattled on and on. On 1 October Rose Woods came to him in great agitation to tell him that a small part of the conversation with Haldeman of 20 June 1972 was missing from the tapes. She thought it was five minutes, but it turned out to be eighteen and a half. In due course this proved one more unpleasant nail in the coffin. Meanwhile, the troubles of Vice-President Agnew were reaching a climax. His prosecution, or at the best resignation, were ever more imminent.

On the day mentioned, 1 October 1973, news reached Nixon that Syria and Egypt were on the verge of launching a major assault on Israel. Neither the American or the Israeli intelligence services had any idea that this was about to happen. The thought naturally occurred to Nixon that the Soviet Union had encouraged the move. The USA at once convened a meeting of the United Nations Security Council.

But Nixon considered that only a battlefield stalemate would make possible a fruitful negotiation.

The situation from his point of view was exceptionally delicate. The United States was recognized to be Israel's prop and stay. The interests of Israel had to be 'kept uppermost'. She could on no account be allowed to go down. But Nixon had been promoting a series of private contacts with Egypt. He hoped that the United States could support the Israelis in such a way that an irreparable break would not be forced with the Egyptians, the Syrians and the other Arab nations. He would also have to restrain the Soviets from intervening in any way that would require a confrontation. These disparate objectives were eventually achieved, if we can judge by the heart-warming reception given next year to Nixon in the Arab States, especially Egypt. But throughout 1973, the tensions were extreme and peace and war, not confined to the Middle East, hung in the balance.

By the fourth day of the war (9 October) the Israelis were having a bad time. If they were to continue fighting, Nixon reckoned that they would need planes and ammunition to replace their early losses. He did not hesitate. He told Kissinger to let the Israelis know that the losses would all be made good by the United States. When he was told that there was disagreement in the Pentagon as to what kind of planes would be used for the airlift, he broke out in exasperation: 'Godammit, tell them to send everything that can fly.' Over the next few weeks there would be more than 550 American missions, more than in the Berlin airlift of 1948.

By 18 October the Israelis were winning the war. The Arabs and their Soviet sponsors began calling for a ceasefire with a surrender by Israel of the territories gained in 1967. This was clearly an unacceptable demand. About the same time the Arabs tried a new form of pressure. The OPEC voted to reduce crude oil production. A number of Arab States imposed total oil embargoes on the United States. A note was received from Brezhnev describing the situation as increasingly dangerous. He suggested that Kissinger come to Moscow immediately. He set off forthwith. Nixon sent a stern message to Brezhnev, but accompanied it with a warm personal greeting which Brezhnev understood and reciprocated.

On 22 October there went into operation in the Middle East a cease-fire drawn up by Kissinger and Brezhnev. There were claims and counter-claims of violation by both sides. A second cease-fire went into effect on 24 October.

But the crisis was by no means over; the worst was still to come. There was an alarming intelligence report of Soviet military and naval moves. A message was received from Brezhnev which Nixon describes today as 'perhaps the most serious threat to US-Soviet relations since the Cuban missile crisis eleven years earlier'. Brezhnev urged that the US and the Soviet Union should each immediately despatch military contingents to the region. He called for an immediate reply and stated that if the Americans did not agree to the joint action proposed, the Soviets would consider acting in a vacuum.

Brezhnev must have known that the idea of a joint American-Russian force could not possibly be accepted by the Americans, who must see in it a Russian device to reinstate their military position in Egypt. Their threat of unilateral action meant therefore a confrontation eyeball to eyeball. Nixon called together his top-level defence advisers. They unanimously recommended that all American and conventional nuclear forces should be put on military alert. In the early morning hours the word was flashed to American bases, installations and naval units in the United States and throughout the world.

Nixon sent at the same time a firm but conciliatory letter to Brezhnev and a personal message to Sadat. The idea of an augmented international force was accepted. The crisis passed. Nixon's performance was a classic feat of top-level diplomacy, the velvet hand and the iron glove working in unison.

On 5 November, Kissinger began the first of many journeys to the Middle East in which he guided Israel and Egypt, and then Israel and Syria towards a peaceful settlement. On 7 November 1973, after six years of estrangement, the United States and Egypt resumed diplomatic relations.

Brezhnev's reaction was delayed till the end of November, but when it came it was cordial. After indicating a willingness to pick up the dialogue of détente, he closed with a personal reference that must be thought genuine. 'We would like, so to say,' he wrote to Nixon, 'to wish you in a personal human way energy and success in overcoming all sorts of complexities, the causes of which are not too easy to understand at a distance.'

By the end of October, self-satisfaction was not likely to be a besetting temptation for Nixon. Too many unpleasant things had happened at home. There had been the resignation of Agnew on 10 October under conditions mentioned earlier. There had been the dismissal of Archibald Cox, the Special Prosecutor (20 October). By 23 October there were twenty-three resolutions for Nixon's impeachment in various stages of discussion on Capitol Hill.

It never seemed possible, looking back, that Archibald Cox could have survived as Special Prosecutor while Nixon remained President. Nixon calls him in his memoirs 'a viper planted in our bosom' – strong language, but understandable when one recalls the passionate enthusiasm with which his young anti-Nixonite lawyers set to work to destroy the President. There is no point in blaming Cox for his predispositions. The responsibility was that of Elliot Richardson who appointed him, and gave him, under pressure from Congress, an unlimited area of investigation. This is not to say that Nixon found an adequate reason for dismissing Cox. His successor as Special Prosecutor, Leon Jaworski, points out that the courts supported Cox's demands for a number of crucial tapes, whereupon Nixon fired him – that is no doubt how the public were entitled to see the matter. Nixon in his memoirs describes at some length his attempts to reach a compromise. Richardson, Cox's superior, seemed ready to accept it, but Cox refused. Dismissal duly followed.

The uproar – what Haldeman called the fire-storm – which followed the dismissal of Cox put in the shade that attending the resignation of Haldeman and Ehrlichman. 'The reaction that evening', in Theodore White's words, 'was as near instantaneous as it had been at Pearl Harbor, or the day of John Kennedy's assassination – an explosion as unpredictable and as sweeping as mass hysteria.' Nixon had not realized till then the depth of the impact that Watergate had been having on America. Yet few statesmen would have stood up as well as he did to the extraordinary combination of strains which he underwent in October 1973.

As the dust settled, the situation for Nixon deteriorated further. The new Special Prosecutor, Leon Jaworski, secured by the charm and skill of General Haig, was an eminent sixty-year-old criminal lawyer from Texas and a former president of the American Bar. Haig told Nixon that Jaworski, though a Democrat, could be relied upon to be objective, i.e. not prejudiced against Nixon. But for once Haig's homework had been defective.

Jaworski pointed out to Haig that on 3 May he had spoken very plainly with Watergate in mind to his fellow attorneys. 'I had', he tells us in his book (*The Right and the Power*) 'lauded Judge John Sirica for his plain and unadulterated faithfulness to duty, which appears to be lacking in some other public servants.... I had recommended that "with dispatch there should be instituted investigatory proceedings assuring a full and fair exposure of all aspects of this incredible affair..." and I had praised the news media for an "alert and astute exposure that sounded a much-needed alarm to the American people...".' There was not likely to be much objectivity in a Special Prosecutor who had made his own position so plain in advance. Haig, however, grasped at him desperately. It had become a more or less impossible task to find someone who would reassure public opinion and at the same time provide fair play for the White House.

Jaworski records with evident satisfaction that his young assistants had already accomplished much to be proud of. Their work had produced guilty pleas from John Dean, the former White House counsel; Jeb Magruder, deputy campaign director of CREEP and former aide to Bob Haldeman; and Fred LaRue, also a CREEP deputy director and aide to John Mitchell, who headed CREEP. All had been charged with conspiring to obstruct justice in the alleged Watergate cover-up. And all had agreed to make full revelations of what they knew about the Watergate case and other operations under investigation.

Yet Jaworski assures us, and we must take his word for it, that it came as a shattering blow to him to read the White House tapes in mid-December. He concluded that the

President of the United States had engaged in highly improper practices – in what appeared to be criminal practices. Jaworski tells us that he had not come to Washington expecting this. He had expected to find all sorts of wrong-doing by Nixon's aides, but it had never occurred to him that the President was 'in the driver's seat'. Jaworski's innocence is surprising when one bears in mind the intense criticism already focused on Nixon personally, including the twenty-three motions of impeachment. Be that as it may, Jaworski was henceforth an implacable antagonist of the President.

In late 1973 Nixon was beginning to think that nothing worse could happen, 'and then something did' – a virulent and well-orchestrated campaign was levelled against his personal financial integrity, especially in regard to his taxes. In the whole grisly story nothing caused him more pain or so much pain to his wife. The details are very complicated. Nixon asked that the joint congressional committee on internal revenue and taxation should investigate the issues.

In the event, in March 1974, Nixon was cleared of any fraud or impropriety. But it was held that (acting on professional advice) he had made unwarranted tax reductions which he was called to repay to the tune of $400,000. In the eyes of the public, it was one more count of guilty.

Nixon had written in his diary at the end of 1972: '1973 will be a better year.' Now, on 23 December 1973, he scribbled the shrewder reflection: 'Last Christmas here?'

12

The Gale of the World
January–August 1974

At the beginning of 1974 Nixon realized that he was about to embark on the campaign of his life. As always, he analysed dispassionately his possible courses of action. He asked himself the basic question: 'Do I fight all-out or do I begin the long process to prepare for a change meaning – in effect, resignation?' He found little difficulty in reaching an answer: 'Fight.' He set down a list of tactical priorities and assessed this piece of self-admonition 'Style: (1) Confidence; (2) Compassion; (3) Colour – the necessity to be interesting. Be strong against unprecedented adversity but avoid intemperate remarks or conduct.' No one can deny the existence in this private entry of a moral, in addition to a political, purpose.

At last he had a striking if short-lived triumph. On 30 January he set off with Pat to deliver the State of the Union address. They had no idea what sort of reception awaited them, but as soon as he entered the chamber door there was a loud 'almost raucous' burst of applause and cheers. Nixon had quite a good story to tell about his stewardship. In the five years of the Nixon administration, domestic discord had been substantially diminished. The cities were now quiet; the college campuses had once again become seats of learning; the rise in crime had been checked; the drug problem had been massively attacked, abroad as well as at home; the draft had been eliminated; and he had submitted to Congress the nation's first environmental programme, as well as major plans for national health care, education reform, revenue-sharing, and government reorganization. He held out an encouraging prospect for 1974.

As he proceeded, Nixon was surprised and moved by the warmth of the reception. He experienced unexpectedly one moment of real glory. He was referring to his overriding aim of establishing a new structure of peace in the world and added: 'This has been and will remain my first priority and the chief legacy I hope to leave from the eight years of my presidency.' Suddenly 'the rafters seemed to ring'. Almost all the Republicans and even a number of Democrats were on their feet applauding and cheering. He looked up to his family. They were beaming – the first time for a long while that they'd had so much to beam about, and the last for a long time to come.

Nixon concluded on an extempore and personal fashion in a hushed chamber. He recognized that the House judiciary committee had a responsibility to investigate Watergate. He would co-operate to the uttermost as long as he was asked to do nothing that would weaken the office of the President. 'Like every member of the House and Senate assembled here tonight, I was elected to the office that I hold. And like every member of the House and Senate, when I was elected to that office, I knew that I was elected for the purpose of doing a job and doing it as well as I possibly can. And I want you to know that I have no intention whatever of ever walking away from the job that the people elected me to do for the people of the United States.'

There was a ring of defiance there, justified surely by the ovation that greeted his earlier reference to the eight years of his presidency. He ended on a note with which no one could quarrel. 'But, my colleagues, this I believe: with the help of God, who has blessed this land so richly, with the co-operation of the Congress, and with the support of the American people, we can and will make the year 1974 a year of unprecedented progress toward our goal of building a structure of lasting peace in the world and a new prosperity without war in the United States of America.' Great stuff while it lasted. But the drift downwards never ceased for long.

Life for Nixon was, however, far from being all or mainly

Watergate. The Middle East war had left behind an Arab oil embargo and an energy crisis. Nixon acted with his usual vigour. In March seven of the nine Arab States had called off the embargo.

Meanwhile, the pressure for more and more tapes went on and on. Nixon lacked the political power to tell them all to go and 'jump in the lake'. At the end of April, he tried a rather desperate expedient. He produced a blue book of transcripts from the tapes. But this did nothing to satisfy the wolves. It was indeed a counter-productive effort. The public were sadly disillusioned to read the kind of talk which went on in the White House; large numbers were disgusted. They would no doubt have been equally embarrassed by the conversations of previous presidents, but they had preferred to cherish ideal pictures. On 22 May Nixon at last dug his toes in and said that he would supply no more tapes. He appealed to the Supreme Court against a District Court decision requiring their production. The Supreme Court decision was expected by the end of June (it was reached in July, in the event). At the beginning of June all hope was not yet lost in the White House. The judiciary committee of the House of Representatives had gone some way to discrediting themselves with their obvious partisanship and endless leaking. There seemed to be something of a reaction in favour of the President. Teddy White was offering the opinion that 'things had bottomed out' for Nixon and that the House of Representatives would not vote for impeachment if the vote were taken at that time. On 7 June Nixon resumed writing his diary after a long break. It would be interesting to know why he chose that moment for the resumption. He went over certain mistakes that he'd made in the last year – most palpably the appointment of Richardson as Attorney-General. At the time of writing he had certainly not lost hope of pulling through.

But the world situation, least of all that in the Middle East, did not wait on American domestic politics. By the end of May Kissinger had spent thirty-two days travelling between Jerusalem and Damascus. He was almost spent, but Nixon encouraged him to persevere. What Nixon still calls the 'impossible', an agreement between Israel and Syria, was signed on 31 May. Nixon decided to strike while the iron was hot and to set off immediately for Egypt, Syria, Saudi Arabia and Israel. He was all too well aware that the American press would continue to be far more concerned with Watergate than the Middle East but he was also aware, though this was not his primary motive, that there was at least a chance that he might in this way restore respect for the presidential office, not to mention himself.

Nixon was overwhelmed by the size and enthusiasm of the crowds that welcomed him in Egypt. It was the most tumultuous welcome, he estimates, that any American President has ever received anywhere in the world. As they drove into Cairo, Sadat turned to him and said, with intense feeling, 'This is a great day for Egypt.' Speaking to a group of reporters, he referred to some of the signs he had seen along the route, for example, 'We trust Nixon'; 'President Nixon never gave a word and didn't fulfil it.' Bearing in mind that Nixon's help to Israel had saved the day for that country a few months earlier, a Nixon fresh from a growing demand for his impeachment in America, this tremendous reception was balm to the soul. The reception was only slightly less enthusiastic in other Arab countries.

That in Israel, though warm enough, was the most restrained. Golda Meir, who had shown such uninhibited gratitude to Nixon after the October war, had just fallen from office. Nixon was aware that his Middle East policy was unpopular in many quarters in Israel. He took the opportunity nonetheless to preach a short lecture on the virtues of moderation and reconciliation. The whole trip demonstrated progress made and held out the promise of more to come. But Nixon was not starry-eyed about the effect on his political fortunes. 'We must have gotten some lift from the trip,' he wrote in his diary, 'although it seems almost impossible to break through in the polls. Of course this is not surprising after the terrible banging we are taking.' Nixon had been getting five or six minutes a day on each television network while he was away, compared with eight or ten minutes on Watergate for over a year.

Nixon was soon off again. He left Washington on 25 June for the 1974 Moscow summit. In his opinion 'the most crucial and hardest fought battle of Summit III took place not in Moscow but in Washington' where the activities of the anti-détente forces reached fever pitch as he was ready to leave. The military establishment were terrified less Summit III might actually succeed in producing a limiting of offensive nuclear weapons or a limited nuclear-test ban. The liberals were (rightly) furious at Soviet treatment of the Jews. Many conservatives were anxious to limit trade with the Soviets or ban it altogether. Nixon refused to give way to any of them. All credit to him at a time when his personal position was weakest. He had never expected that Summit III was going to produce any big news as far as new agreements were concerned. Brezhnev, however, was if possible even more friendly than previously. He and Nixon boarded Brezhnev's Soviet yacht for a sail on the Black Sea. Brezhnev put his arm round Nixon and said, 'We must do something of vast historical importance. We want every Russian and every American to be friends that talk to each other as you and I are talking to each other here on this boat.' Cynics will treat all such exchanges as claptrap. Yet, unless we decline to pay the slightest attention to the relationship between world leaders, the friendship, as one must call it, between Brezhnev and Nixon was a bonus mark for peace. It was agreed that there should be a mini-summit before the end of the year. Nixon left hoping that a breakthrough might come about then – if he was spared.

Now it was back to harsh reality in Washington. Nixon heads the next section of his memoirs 'Impeachment Summer'. Week after week one bit of bad news followed another. No one could calculate better than Nixon the actualities of the voting balance in the judiciary committee of the House of Representatives where of course the Democrats had a majority. After a quarter of a century of life in Washington politics, he possessed an intimate knowledge of the factors likely to weigh with each individual. He was less optimistic than most of his less experienced advisors, knowing the form so well.

Looking back, he considers that by the last week of July an underlying political consensus to impeach him had been arrived at. This was before the Supreme Court decision on the remaining tapes had been handed down, and before the deadly tape of 23 June 1972 had been published.

There were heavy blows still to be inflicted and suffered. When it came, the Supreme Court decision was as bad as it could be for Nixon. They decided unanimously that Nixon must surrender the required tapes. As Haig described it to Nixon, 'There's an air in it, it's tight as a drum.' This meant, above all, that the tape of 23 June 1972 would have to be surrendered. Nixon might well appear to have entered into or even initiated a cover-up within a few days of the Watergate break-in. By this time he was searching his soul yet again as to whether it was his duty to resign at once or wait until the House of Representatives had voted for impeachment.

He obtained some satisfaction from finding that he possessed a feeling of calm and strength. 'To a certain extent,' he comments, 'the calmness and strength may have come from somewhere out of my background, perhaps from my father and mother.' He decided not to give in quite yet. But by 29 July, back in Washington, he found that impeachment hysteria had taken over the city. The White House staff was cloaked in gloom. By 30 July the judiciary committee of the House of Representatives had passed three articles of impeachment though they had rejected two relating to Cambodia and Nixon's taxes. On the night of 30 July, he could not get to sleep. He went over and over the arguments for and against resigning, jotting them down on paper in his usual fashion. By the time he had finished it was almost morning. His 'natural instincts welled up'. He turned the paper over and wrote on the back: 'End career as a fighter.'

But the time had passed when sheer courage and willpower could provide a solution. The following morning Haig, who had just read the transcript of the 23 June conversation for the first time, came to tell him that it was all up, that defeat had to be accepted. 'Mr President,' he said, 'I just don't see how we can survive this one.' He mentioned the two closest legal advisors as holding the same view and continued, 'The staff won't hold and public opinion won't hold either, once this tape gets out.' On the following day, 1 August, Nixon told Haig that he had decided to resign. If the 23 June tape was not explainable he could not very well expect the staff to try to explain and defend it. A week was to pass before the resignation took effect but the crucial decision had been taken.

Nixon in his memoirs quotes at length from the moving diary kept by his daughter Tricia. The attitude of his family did not in the end alter history but they made a whole world of difference to Nixon at that time and their indomitable love for him should weigh heavily in his favour. A few extracts are all that can be given here. On 2 August, Tricia records, Julie called her to Washington. She walked into Julie's room and found her on the telephone. 'Seeing me, she disengaged herself. I calmly asked her what Daddy had said to her yesterday. "He thinks he must resign." "Why?" "Because he has virtually no support left." "Julie I can't believe this isn't a nightmare. It cannot be happening."' Pat Nixon had not yet been told. They broke the news to her: 'I was still trying to protect Mama and spare her from grief. Daddy of course is always protective of everyone but himself.' Happy the man of whom *in extremis* that could be written by his daughter. She went in to see her father. He began a clear description of the 23 June tape and an analysis of his position. 'I only interrupted when he began to speak of resigning for the good of the country. I told him for the good of the country he must stay in office. Then as I was leaving I went over to where he was, put my arms around him, kissed his forehead, and without warning I burst into tears and said brokenly, "You are the most decent person I know." Emotions for me are usually completely controllable externally. But when Daddy said, "I hope I have not let you down," the tragedy of his ghastly position shattered me.'

Nixon next took a step that must have cost him a good deal, but there was a good deal of pain about. He insisted that his family should read the fateful and fatal 23 June tape for themselves. They did so, and returned to the Lincoln Sitting-room. 'Ed, Julie and I came out strongly for not resigning. David was less sure. But all of us were in concert in feeling that we wanted Daddy to do what he felt he should. . . . We left Daddy alone in his chair, staring into the fire. . . . Upstairs, Mama, Ed and I went to the third floor to say good night to Julie and David. We all broke down together and put our arms around each other in circular huddle-style fashion, saying nothing.'

Nixon's decision to resign wavered under the impact of his family's devout resolution. He decided to give his presidency one last throw. He would wait till the public had had a chance to read the 23 June tape before making an irrevocable decision. But that postponement inevitably led to nothing. When the tape was published on 3 August the reaction was as bad as predicted. The Cabinet, it is true, still held firm in Nixon's recollection. Nixon presided over them on 6 August without announcing his resignation.

The ex-President gives a dead-pan account of that Cabinet meeting. Ford in his memoirs brings out the drama and the pathos. He had assumed that this was going to be a momentous occasion, that Nixon was going to come to grips with the threat to his presidency and set out clearly his future course of action. Instead he started out with a dissertation on the economy. But before the end he had come round to Watergate. Ford sat directly across the table from him; he remembers thinking how tired and drawn Nixon looked. 'The consensus now is that we'll lose in the House,' he said, referring to the impeachment debate that was scheduled to begin on 15 August. 'But I want all the facts out. I'll take whatever lumps are involved. After consulting with people more knowledgable than I am about constitution law, I am convinced that there is no evidence of an impeachable offence. If there were, I wouldn't stay in this office one more day.' No one was any clearer at the end than they had been at the beginning as to whether he meant to resign. But afterwards he told Kissinger that he meant to do so. The latter was forced to agree 'as a friend' that Nixon was choosing the right course, but 'I begged him to stay on to help Gerald Ford who would automatically succeed him'.

Then Nixon went on with much apprehension to break the news to his family. He need not have been quite so anxious. 'My wife and daughters remained an indomitable trio. Each one respected the opportunities public life had given her; and when the blows came each reacted with dignity, courage and spirit.' One more talk with Kissinger rounded off the day.

They went over present relationships with the Chinese and the Soviets and about problems in the Middle East, in Europe and in other parts of the world. They reminisced about the decisions of the past five and a half years. Nixon found himself more emotional at the end than he had been at any time since the decision to resign.

Then came an incident for which Nixon was much derided at the time by his enemies but which, in my eyes, does him nothing but honour. On an impulse he told Kissinger how every night when he had finished work in the Lincoln Sitting-room, he would stop and kneel briefly. 'Following my mother's Quaker custom, I would pray silently for a few minutes before going to bed. I asked him to pray with me now, and we knelt.'

At 4.30 on Wednesday 7 August, he was visited by Gold-water, Scott and Rhodes; Goldwater as the elder statesman of the Republican party, Scott their (minority) leader in the Senate and Rhodes their (minority) leader in the House of Representatives. Nixon and Goldwater have given their accounts since and in harmony. The delegations brought home to Nixon the fact that the situation was hopeless in the Senate, that impeachment would certainly succeed there, that he could not rely on more than sixteen or eighteen votes. It was brought home to Nixon that Goldwater, Scott and Rhodes, his long-time supporters, would all vote for impeachment under one heading at least. But with wisdom and sensitivity, the visitors did not demand that Nixon should resign. They were well aware that that might be counter-productive. They left him to make his own decision in the light of the horrific facts. Goldwater was by now painfully disillusioned. As he writes himself, he was in no mood to forgive Nixon for his past actions. But he says this today deliberately: 'I did believe and I do believe that in this, his final hour of agony, he was putting the welfare of the nation ahead of every other consideration.'

When the party left Nixon, he had still not declared his intentions. But Goldwater, by no means tender towards Nixon in connection with Watergate, tells us that the magnitude of the situation brought tears to his eyes. 'The President knew what he must do. Thank God he did not require us to spell out the message we carried. When we left he was smiling. Whatever else I may say or think about Richard Nixon, he displayed a quality of courage I have rarely encountered on that Wednesday afternoon.'

Thursday 8 August 1974 was the last full day Richard Nixon served as President. First he saw Gerry Ford and wished him all that was good. Ford himself describes the scene. 'Nixon', he says, 'was sitting behind his desk, but he stood up as soon as I entered.' They shook hands. 'Sit down,' said the President. Ford took the chair to his right. Nixon leant back with his hands clasped together, his face was solemn. He had been under tremendous strain; he was still very tense, but in control. Speaking slowly and deliberately, he came right to the point. 'I have made the decision to resign,' he said. 'It's in the best interest of the country. I won't go into the details pro and con. I have made my decision.' He paused for a moment, then added: 'Gerry, I know you'll do a good job.'

'Mr President,' I replied, 'you know that I'm saddened by this circumstance. I would have wanted it to be otherwise, but I am ready to do the job and think I'm fully qualified to do it.' Nixon replied, 'I know you are, too.'

That said, Nixon relaxed. The conversation was as pleasant as it could be in the circumstances. In Ford's words, 'Now that he had relinquished the burdens of the world, he was offering an old friend the best advice available for the days ahead.'

Later Nixon saw Haig and Ziegler and said something from the depths of his character. He did not care what people thought as long as they did not think he had quit just because things were tough. 'How can you support a quitter? I have never quit before in my life. Maybe this is what none of you has understood this whole time. You don't quit.'

Then he had a meeting with the congressional leaders, who seemed relatively unmoved. Then he went into the Cabinet room. Forty-six men were crowded round the table and in the chairs along the walls. He spoke about the great tasks they had performed together, but a six months' trial in the Senate was too long for the country.... Now it was Gerry Ford they must support with their votes, their affections and their prayers. The emotional level in the room was almost unbearable. 'I just hope that I haven't let you down,' was his final message.

There were two more public performances to be got through. The broadcast to the nation reads well today. Many were to be found at that time, and can be found still, to criticize the absence of remorse, but he did not feel that he had committed a sin in the moral sense and to have pretended to one would have been much less creditable. He treated the decision to resign in quite a matter-of-fact fashion: 'In the last few days it has become evident to me that I no longer have a strong enough political base in the Congress to justify continuing in office.' Then he delivered what he calls the most difficult sentence he has ever had or will ever have to speak. Looking directly into the camera, he said: 'Therefore I shall resign the presidency effective at noon tomorrow.' He continued: 'By taking this action, I hope that I will have hastened the start of that process of healing which is so desperately needed in America.'

'I regret deeply any injuries that may have been done in the course of the events that led to this decision. I would say only that if some of my judgments were wrong – and some were wrong – they were made in what I believed at the time to be in the best interest of the nation.' And he concluded: 'To have served in this office is to have felt a very personal sense of kinship with each and every American. In leaving it, I do so with this prayer: May God's grace be with you in the days ahead.'

Next day there was an occasion which was bound to be the most emotional of all. He and his family made their way to the East Room for the final meeting with the administration officials, Cabinet members and White House staff. The announcement was made: 'Ladies and gentlemen, the President of the United States of America and Mrs Nixon; Mr and Mrs Edward Cox; Mr and Mrs David Eisenhower' – normal. Then: thunderous applause; scraping of chairs as people rose to their feet; 'Hail to the Chief!' The emotion in the room, records Nixon, was overpowering, even more so than in the Cabinet room the day before. For some minutes Nixon could not quieten the applause. Many of the faces were filled with tears. For me personally what followed, as it comes down to us, possesses its own beauty, but of course anti-Nixonites will go on treating it as a crude exploitation of sentiment. It seems inevitable to quote one passage in full: 'I remember my old man. I think that they would have called him a sort of a little man, common man. He didn't consider himself that way. You know what he was? He was a streetcar motorman first, and then he was a farmer, and then he had a lemon ranch. It was the poorest lemon ranch in California, I can assure you. He sold it before they found oil on it. And then he was a grocer. But he was a great man because he did his job, and every job counts up to the hilt, regardless of what happens.' He went on to speak of what was still more sacred: 'Nobody will ever write a book, probably, about my mother. Well, I guess all of you would say this about your mother; my mother was a saint. And I think of her, two boys dying of tuberculosis, nursing four others in order that she could take care of my older brother for three years in Arizona, and seeing each of them die, and when they died, it was like one of her own. Yes, she will have no books written about her. But she was a saint.' There is one other ineluctable quotation. 'Always', he concluded, 'give your best, never get discouraged; always remember others may hate you, but those who hate you don't win unless you hate them, and then you destroy yourself.' No doubt Richard Nixon did not live up to those words. Which of us has ever done so? But we shall never appreciate him fairly, unless we recognize that they expressed an essential part of the man.

Soon it was all over. They were in the air. The people on the ground below were waving. They too disappeared. There was no talk among the passengers. They were numbed with exhaustion and sadness.

13
'They Gave Me a Sword'

Nixon refers to 'the four truths about Watergate – the factual, the legal, the moral and the political'. Even this list of headings is not exhaustive. Take Elliot Richardson's summing-up, for example (in *The Creative Balance*):

Knowing all that I know now I think I can discern three principal contributory ingredients. One was Richard Nixon's own distrustful style, a compound both of his personal insecurity and of his reaction to the reality of bitter attack. A second was the amoral alacrity to do his bidding of a politically inexperienced, organization-minded staff, obsessively driven by the compulsion to win. A third was the aggrandizement of the presidential power and the tendencies towards its abuse that had already been set in motion before Nixon took office.

I suppose that that might be called an historical verdict, though not in my eyes fair to Nixon. It comes a trifle strangely from a distinguished upright man who accepted office more than once under Nixon and actually became his Attorney-General when Kleindienst, the existing incumbent, resigned at the same time as Haldeman and Ehrlichman (30 April 1973).

The factual account given by Nixon in his extensive memoirs has not, as far as I can see, been challenged even by hostile critics. No leading statesman has ever been so completely exposed. The endless investigations and the unprecedented publication of the tapes have made sure of that. His personal narrative is likely to survive for all times as substantially accurate as far as it goes. The legal issue, in so far as it concerns Nixon, was never brought to a final conclusion. That was averted by his resignation and the pardon given him by President Ford. He himself, a very successful lawyer, has always insisted that he did not infringe the criminal law. Plenty of other lawyers have said the opposite. The chances of his receiving a fair trial seemed always remote. It becomes unreal to speculate what would have happened in a law court of strict justice. An impeachment, an essentially political process, would not have proved the legal point one way or another.

The fact remains, however, that those who were closest to him politically went to jail: Mitchell, his best friend in politics, Haldeman, Ehrlichman and Colson among them. One would have to be an unqualified supporter of the former President to claim that he remained throughout on the right side of the law.

When we turn to the 'political truth', we soon find that the political and moral factors are intertwined. Watergate was, in truth, the greatest failure in the history of American politics – far more complete even than that of President Wilson after Versailles. Nixon's political opponents, above all the most influential media, played a large part in bringing about his destruction. But he himself has not shrunk from accepting, as he must, heavy blame. 'I screwed it up,' as he said at the Oxford Union. Or, in the words he used to David Frost: 'I gave them a sword and they stuck it in' – to which he added, not ungenerously, that he would have done the same in their place. In this supreme political examination, the lifelong master of the art of politics achieved an omega mark.

Amid all the flood of books and articles on Nixon, I think that we shall approach the truth if we focus on two books in particular: *The Right and the Power* (1976) by Leon Jaworski, who succeeded Archibald Cox as Special Prosecutor; and *With Nixon* (1977) by Raymond Price, Nixon's speech writer and intimate associate from 1968 to the end of his presidency. 'Wise, balanced, leaning to the liberal side', in Kissinger's description, Ray Price has set a fine example of fidelity. Jaworski's book is described by Nixon's arch enemy the *Wash-*

ington Post as 'the most powerful and consequential book about Watergate that has yet to be written'. It is, as one might expect, a prosecutor's indictment. Price's book is described by the publishers as 'drawing a picture of the Nixon years which is, on balance, sympathetic': a fair comment. Price candidly distinguishes a good Nixon, a morally neutral Nixon (legitimately Machiavellian) and a bad Nixon. The fact that Price served him right to the end of his presidency and is working for him again today demonstrates that, in his eyes, the essential Nixon has always been the good one. After his fall, he found an occasion to launch into a long Dutch-uncle lecture about his bad side (his actual distinction is between Nixon's 'light' and his 'dark' side). 'The point I tried to drive home was that he could acknowledge the dark side, deal with it without losing the support or the faith of those who were still his friends. He would not be telling us anything that we had not already counted 'into the equation.'

Price saw some of the tension drain away. At one point Nixon looked out of the window, then turned back again, grinned and commented: 'Of course it's true. We could never have brought off the opening to China if we hadn't lied a little, could we?' Nixon, in that remark, did not perhaps go all the way with Price's analysis, but he made a healthy beginning.

For Jaworski, Nixon by the end of his presidency had only a dark side, though 'he had thought that Nixon would make a good and strong President'. He became instead 'petty and arrogant, determined to use the powers of his office as he pleased, whether right or wrong.... How different', he goes on, 'might have been the course of government if there had been an acknowledgment of God as the source of right instead of a denial of Him in a seemingly unending series of ruthless actions.' I am ready to believe that Jaworski is himself a religious man, though not above colloguing with representatives of *Time* magazine, in a successful attempt 'to get on the cover'. He was there following the still more successful example of Judge Sirica who managed to become 'Man of the Year' in 1973 after a dinner with the top executives of *Time*. (See David Halberstam, *The Powers That Be*, pages 692–4). The leading critics of the President would not appear on balance to have been as religious as Nixon himself. When, in the last awful moments of his presidency, he asked Kissinger to join him in prayer, the story was widely circulated as a suitable matter for derision.

What Jaworski does not do is to compare Nixon's performance before and after Watergate with the performance of former Presidents in similar areas. Jaworski and his team of eager young prosecutors did not have the exciting opportunity of examining these past Presidents or their acolytes. It becomes necessary, however, to go into this question of whether Nixon and his men did or did not do anything worse than their predecessors.

Here, as always, we must begin by distinguishing between (1) the background of Watergate, (2) Watergate itself and (3) its aftermath, including the cover-up. There is nothing in pre-Nixon days to compare with the elaborateness of this same cover-up, with the evasiveness and in some cases downright lying of 'the conspirators', as Jaworski would have called them. But who knows to what former Presidents would have resorted, if they, like Nixon, or their acolytes had been caught with their hand in the till? This takes us to the background of Watergate. We are left to compare the morals of the Nixon White House with earlier conduct and finding a close comparison barely possible.

In November 1978 Chuck Colson, as already mentioned, came to London to address an embryo Christian Fellowship which some of us are trying to found under the inspiration of his own great initiative in America. I asked him in a talk after the conference, but in a Christian context: 'Would you say in retrospect that your dirty tricks [I meant all those connected, however remotely, with Nixon] were any worse than the dirty tricks employed under earlier Presidents?' He paused for reflection and gave a considered answer: 'No, I really don't think so, though all such dirty tricks are lamentable.'

David Frost cannot fairly be accused of being soft in his interrogation of Nixon, though he paints an attractive picture of him towards the end. But even before his interviews with Nixon began, he was aware that previous administrations had done some very strange things, which must be understood if

Nixon's conduct was to be placed in perspective. Perhaps the list quoted by Frost will seem less biased in Nixon's favour than one from Victor Lasky, whose arresting book *It Did Not Start with Watergate* has not been refuted:

For about twenty years, the CIA and, for a lesser period, the FBI had conducted mail covers and inspection of letters addressed to or by US citizens.

Wiretaps of US citizens without court warrants had been commonplace at least since the 1930s. Indeed, the number of national security wiretaps conducted during Nixon's administration was lower than under any President since Franklin Roosevelt.

Warrantless room bugging – the so-called black-bag jobs – had been conducted by the FBI and CIA since World War II. Burglaries had also been commonplace.

Embarrassing personal information on political foes had been sent by the FBI to a number of Presidents, again beginning with F.D.R.

CIA and FBI infiltration into domestic political groups was extensive under Johnson.

CIA excesses against foreign nations and leaders were also well documented in earlier administrations.

It can be urged against Nixon that the plumbers, his 'special police force' of four persons operating for several months, was an unpleasant novelty of his own. But even after Arthur Schlesinger's eloquent eulogy of Robert Kennedy, it is impossible not to associate the Kennedys with plans to assassinate Castro – a more horrible idea, surely, than anything actually perpetrated by Nixon.

In the absence of investigations into the activities of previous Presidents in these areas, it will always be impossible to strike a just balance. But, and this is important, Nixon could and can reasonably believe that his White House was no worse in these respects than those of his predecessors. Believing that, it would have been sheer humbug for him to express the kind of remorse that his critics yearned for and present himself on his knees as a unique sinner among American Presidents. Would any of us really think the better of him for doing so?

Let us leave out speculative comparisons with other Presidents where evidence is very inconclusive. If Nixon can be held to have brought about his own downfall, I would say that the cause lay in the atmosphere he allowed to emerge in his entourage in the year or two before the break-in. And yet that same atmosphere could so easily have *not* produced the break-in. He could have run his course with just a little good fortune and gone down in history with a glorious record.

Chuck Colson would not seem to agree with this assessment. He has many kindly things to say about Nixon, but according to him *hubris* became the mark of the Nixon man ... 'We set in motion forces that would sooner or later make Watergate or something like it inevitable.'

I am not bound to agree here with my friend Chuck Colson who is perhaps unconsciously purging himself of the sinfulness of his own involvement. The distinction between what was or was not legal for a President was, in view of past presidential activities, nothing like so clear-cut for 1972 as Safire postulates. 'The root decision', he tells us, 'from which so much else followed, to put in the wire-taps on newsmen, was Nixon's, with Kissinger, Haig, Mitchell, Ehrlichman and Haldeman right with him.' Does anyone suggest that Kissinger and Haig would or should have been prosecuted if their part had been uncovered? Certainly the 'win at all costs' atmosphere in the White House created the distinct possibility of a Watergate. To say that the one made the other *inevitable* seems to me an unjustified hypothesis. But once Watergate had been exposed to the public eye, the existence of the previous 'dirty tricks' greatly magnified the temptation to cover up the Watergate exercise.

Once Watergate had happened, could not Nixon, the master of political strategy and tactics, the great survivor who had emerged from so many other predicaments, have found the way out of this one?

For the first six months of the Watergate episode, Nixon was absorbed in many pressing affairs, especially the election itself. But not only the election. Apart from all the ordinary duties of a President, there was China, there was Russia, there was the Middle East and, above all, the intensive struggle for peace in Vietnam. These exertions can fairly be regarded as a counter-weight of achievement to set against the appalling failure over Watergate. They are also to some extent an explanation of how Nixon came to make the total Watergate misjudgment, particularly in the early stages. And, of course, bad luck came into it on a mighty scale. Nixon himself does not, however, moan about bad luck. As already mentioned, he 'screwed it up'. His mistake was a 'beaut' – 'I let everybody down.' On this showing, his major error, perhaps his sole error, occurred *after* the break-in, but at that point what else could he have done? He could, as David Frost has recognized, have pardoned the Watergate delinquents on the wave of his election victory. Was he too proud and, if so, in a good or a less good sense? We certainly, and he probably, will never know.

Nixon himself says today he should have immediately taken steps to discover and prosecute the guilty persons. But at what point in time should these steps have been taken? Price says that it is the conventional wisdom that he should have got to the bottom of the matter at once, discovered Mitchell's responsibility and dismissed the latter. But he says rightly that this was psychologically impossible for Nixon. As he puts it vividly:

So – was he going to blow the whistle and send John Mitchell, his friend, confidant, law partner, campaign manager, Attorney-General, to prison at the age of fifty-nine? For being somehow involved in bugging the Democratic National Committee headquarters, when Nixon himself was convinced that he had been bugged by Johnson in 1968? When he had felt it necessary to have his own campaign headquarters in 1968 swept for bugs every week? No – or at least, this is my guess – he damn well was not. He was going to do what F.D.R. probably would have done, or Johnson or Kennedy or Harry Truman. He was going to do what he could to make the whole mess go away – to contain it, limit the political damage, to keep it from reaching Mitchell if Mitchell were involved.

Nixon is surely right (though it is not the whole truth) in saying to David Frost that he allowed his heart to rule his head. This failure to tackle Mitchell may be put down either to loyalty or to moral timidity, or to a fear that Mitchell knew too much.

The stricter moralists will not be satisfied with the account, no doubt entirely sincere, that he gives in his memoirs for not acting drastically when he first heard of the Watergate break-in. He thought it extraordinarily silly, but did not see anything particularly immoral about it. That kind of thing was familiar enough in American elections. He refused to get morally worked up about it. Does one denounce him for his frankness? Does anyone argue that previous American Presidents would have felt any genuine moral indignation over this episode? Fortunately for themselves, they were never placed in this particular situation.

Let us assume, however, that Nixon showed a perhaps human reluctance to tackle Watergate when it first surfaced at the end of June 1972. He persuaded himself that it might well go away. He had of course special reasons in that electoral year for playing it down. But when in November he was renewed as President with an immense majority, then, as Colson, for example, told me as described, was surely the time to tackle it intensively. As mentioned earlier, Nixon was so pre-occupied with Vietnam that he let the crucial month of January go by. He continued to shirk the issue.

By 21 March 1973 when Nixon had his fateful conversation with Dean, it was almost too late. If he had come clean then and admitted to everything he knew, it is just possible that he could have got away with it. But he was already by that time in the toils. On 23 March Judge Sirica announced that McCord, one of the actual break-in men, had confessed that political pressure had been brought to bear on him to plead guilty. And from that moment, the hunt was in full cry.

By that time Nixon had already, in retrospect, 'screwed it up', although he continued President for another eighteen months, with considerable benefit to the free world. There were, even if Jaworski cannot understand this, other nobler impulses at work in him than that of pure survivalism, though they were powerful enough. The institution of the presidency, the interest of the American people and world peace were all factors working in him potently.

Up to this point I have barely mentioned the tapes. Many will argue that if he had never bugged himself, or if he had at least destroyed the tapes before it was too late, he would somehow have scraped through. Faced with such profound hostility from Congress and the media, and later the judiciary, I cannot believe that he could have come out on top. He might in a nominal sense have survived as President, but he would in any case have failed totally to achieve his lofty presidential aims. In theory two courses were open to him: (1) in, say, January 1973, to get to the bottom of the whole business and make sure the guilty were prosecuted, or (2) to do precisely the opposite and pardon them all. In practice, I cannot believe there would have been much future in either course.

We are left with the conclusion that he was very unlucky that Watergate should have occurred at all, however dangerous an atmosphere he had created. Once Watergate had occurred, it must always have been very hazardous to expose the guilty, because they could turn round and say that they had had plenty of encouragement, indirectly at least, from him. To show them clemency would have been to attempt the ascent of a slippery slope leading to endless investigation and unremitting exposure. Possibly in the end it was inevitable that American presidential politics, ever more ruthlessly competitive, would produce a personal tragedy of this kind. Bill Gulley (*Breaking Cover*) served under four Presidents at the strategical centre of the White House, the military office, and apparently has a good idea of what went on in the White House previously. He writes: 'You never worried about the law ... my thinking was, if the President wants it done, it's right. I never questioned it. It never occurred to me that some sheriff might show up some day with a warrant.' If it had not been Nixon, it might well have been his successor. In that sense, and in that sense only, Nixon did not suffer in vain.

14
The Man and the Warning

Richard Nixon, wrote David Frost after their television discussions, longed so much to be great. No one who has read
Nixon's memoirs, particularly the diary entries scattered
throughout the thousand pages, would dispute the perci-
pience of that assessment. Such a longing is shared by most
of those who have achieved the heights in politics, apart from
countless lesser mortals; by John Kennedy certainly and, after
his death, by his brother Robert; by Winston Churchill and
subsequent British Prime Ministers, with the exception I
would suggest of Lord Attlee (truly great in my eyes) and Sir
Alec Douglas-Home. I cannot be disparaged as an unworthy
aspiration.

In the case of Richard Nixon, the dream was more articu-
lated than usual. On 9 January 1965 he wrote down eight New
Year's resolutions of which the first was 'Set great goals', and
he went a long way before his political downfall to live up
to that purpose. At the time of his resignation, the *New York
Times* produced a kind of omnibus volume seeking to provide
a background to the whole subject. None of the writers was
remotely kind to Nixon. But the chapter on the resignation,
by R. W. Apple, contains this passage which provides at least
some element of balance: 'Almost forgotten by the time Mr
Nixon tendered his resignation were his days of glory when
he began dismantling the cold war that had dominated American politics for a quarter-century, with his dramatic journeys

to Peking and Moscow and the signing of the first limitation on the deadly nuclear arms race. Almost forgotten were his successes in ending American involvement in the bitterly divisive Vietnam war and in halting the draft.' R. W. Apple did well at that moment to recall the facts mentioned.

But nothing can remove another fact from American history – that Richard Nixon was the first President to be forced to resign under threat of impeachment. The hounds were on his trail within a few months of his winning an almost record victory in the 1972 election. When he was under heavy assault, a friend tried to console him by suggesting that Lincoln had had a still worse press in his day. Nixon remarked wryly, 'I'm catching up,' a comment which would have been appreciated by Lord Attlee and, for that matter, Sir Winston Churchill. He finished by setting up new records for the amount of opprobrium heaped on a President.

No one has all it takes to be a statesman, not even Sir Winston Churchill, most admired of British statesmen in this century. But he had a good deal of it always, as did Attlee and Macmillan. So, for example, did John Kennedy potentially. So did Richard Nixon. On the domestic side it was hard to judge Nixon. His administrative plans made a great deal of sense. It was not only his right but his duty to sort out the vast incoherent bureaucracy in the interests of efficient presidential government. His attempts, however, to move government away from Washington and at the same time to enhance the influence of the President over the whole field were bound to encounter strong resistance from Congress. His social philosophy based on self-help, beyond all other conceptions, will strike British readers as bearing a strong resemblance to that of Mrs Thatcher, British Prime Minister at the time of writing.

In each case there is a reference back to the ideals of the non-conformist shop-keeper, whether in America or England. Nixon's father, as mentioned earlier, though a poor man, would never make use of the benefits of State medicine for his much-loved dying son. Self-help as an expression of the Christian ethic provides its own integrity, which will be challenged and reasserted to the end of time. But Mrs Thatcher possesses one great advantage over President Nixon in a secure parliamentary majority. As we are well aware by now, he had Congress continuously against him. Of the first forty measures he brought before Congress, only two were passed. On the home front, his dream of far-reaching conservative reforms never had much of a chance. What little chance they had was destroyed not only by Watergate but by the deteriorating economic situation, which baffled equally the President, his advisers and his enemies.

It is on the international side that Nixon's longing to be great came somewhere near fulfilment. 'China was now an important friend,' writes Kissinger. 'We built a new basis for stable relations with the Soviet Union through the Berlin agreement, the first strategic arms limitation treaty and an agreed code of international conduct.' The diplomatic revolution, coupled with a new balanced policy in the Middle East opened up what Kissinger calls an extraordinary opportunity for American diplomacy.

Kissinger will go to his grave convinced that all these great achievements precariously attained would have been made permanent if the executive authority of the presidency had not been overthrown by the events connected with Watergate. Be that unprovable hypothesis true or false, the services to world peace of the Nixon administration have not passed away as though they had never been.

Among so many mishaps, Nixon had good fortune in lighting upon Henry Kissinger as his intimate ally. The manner in which Kissinger spoke about Nixon behind his back has been quite often criticized. Nixon told David Frost that 'it drove my family up the wall', but it didn't seem to worry Nixon. He and Kissinger served each other's purposes and, vastly more important, the wider interests of humanity. During the last emotional crisis, his persuading Kissinger to join him on his knees was surely a mark of unique confidence. In the last resort, Nixon and Kissinger were two men of immensely powerful intellect, dedicated to world peace and joined by an exceptional allegiance to the honour of America. Kissinger tells us movingly in his memoirs what it meant to him, a Jewish refugee from the Nazis, to be accepted as utterly equal in the land of the free. Some such fellow-feeling seemed to pass between Nixon and the returning prisoners-of-war.

This bond seems to me to have been the one which bound them closest.

I have described Nixon as bringing to international policy a global vision, an overall world perspective which he set out to apply in systematic detail. He is not the only post-war statesman for whom that claim could be put forward. It was true of Ernest Bevin, under whom I worked at close quarters for a year. Bevin's world policy became so intricate that at one point he had to await the return of Sir William (later Lord) Strang to England to remind him of all the minutiae. It was no doubt true also of Harold Macmillan. But no post-war statesman had entered into supreme power with so much expert international background as Nixon.

The ex-President can, not unfairly, be referred to as anti-communist, but the phrase can be somewhat misleading. From his first trip to Europe in 1947 until his final personal talk with David Frost, he consistently saw the force of international communism as a permanent deep-rooted threat to the peace and freedom of the world. So, we must think, has it been looked on by all those responsible for Britain's foreign and defence policy since the war. Otherwise the huge expenditure on armaments would be quite beyond explanation. But long before he had become President, his anti-communism had ceased to be aggressive in so far as it ever was. By that time, of course, the split had occurred between Russia and China. When he was welcomed to China by Chou En-lai in 1972, he recalled that, as we have seen, that in 1954 Foster Dulles had refused to shake hands with Chou. Nixon rectified that at once. They both felt that a whole world of mutual hostility had passed away in that moment.

He did not set out to use China merely as an instrument of policy against Soviet Russia. His attitude towards both the great communist countries included personal friendliness and as much free communication, trade and other forms of contact as could be promoted. It also involved a strong American defence system. In that respect America could never relax for a moment. But nothing became him better than his insistence on continuing the struggle for a disarmament agreement as he approached the third summit in 1974. His own military advisers were trying to hold him back at a time when his personal position was on the point of collapse. This in his eyes was an historic moment, even if the fruits would not be gathered till later. In international matters generally, he showed a thorough mastery of his subject, professional timing and strong nerves at moments of crisis.

On Vietnam, the marks awarded Nixon will vary according to the selection of the examiners. I have indicated in the text why I cannot accept the scathing criticism of William Shaw-cross in relation to the Cambodian policy, heavily, if selectively, documented. I must at least concede that the secrecy of the bombing in March 1969 did him more harm than good in the end. He was left by President Johnson with an appalling situation; half a million American troops in Vietnam, thousands of American prisoners in North Vietnamese hands, and little hope of winning the war by any means that would be tolerated by American public opinion. The latter was demanding with increasing savagery the return of the troops.

He hoped on the advice offered him to end the war in a year and in fact it took four years for this to happen. With the steady reduction of the troops, the heavy bombing was the only method left open to him. In the end he secured the return of the prisoners-of-war and a settlement that gave South Vietnam a chance on paper of survival.

Congress took steps to destroy that last possibility. What could or should Nixon have done that was different from what he did? Unconditional withdrawal, leaving the prisoners-of-war to the tender mercies of North Vietnam? Dishonourable in Nixon's eyes, and, I may add, in mine. Much heavier bombing, much sooner, which might well have brought the war to a much more rapid end? Equally immoral in many eyes, politically impossible in the view of almost everyone. Whoever considers that they could have handled the whole issue much better must cast the first stone. But who is qualified for that undertaking?

Nixon's critics have been many and bitter and not a few of them highly gifted. They are reluctant even to allow the word tragedy to be applied to the shattering contrast between his desire for greatness and the pitiful conclusion. They want him to grovel. They go on complaining that he cannot even now realize the extent of his delinquency. We have gone into this in the previous chapter. Some of them sneer at his final prayer session with Kissinger, unable to believe that anything he ever did was not actuated by a political motive.

David Frost (to quote him again) referred also to Nixon's thirst for nobility – another happy phrase. If there is one quality which, in addition to the longing to be great, emerges from his memoirs and diaries, it is the longing to be good, the desire for moral self-improvement. That brings us naturally to his Quaker upbringing, which does not seem to me to have been taken seriously enough by most of those who have written about him. But, as emerges from the first chapter of this book, his formation was exceptionally religious, his life dominated by family, church and school. When he told Kissinger near the end that he said his prayers every night in the White House, it is not only possible to believe him, it is *essential* to believe him to grasp one of the continuing threads which ran from his earliest to his final days.

The memory of his mother, whom he always referred to as a saint, was never far from his thoughts. On the night he was inaugurated as Vice-President (20 January 1953), she handed him, as we have seen, a small piece of paper on which she had written this message:

To Richard:
You have gone far and we are proud of you always – I know that you will keep your relationship with your maker as it should be for after all that, as you must know, is the most important thing in this life.

But the ideal of saintliness was not the only one inculcated in him from early beginnings. His father was combative. Richard became excessively combative. Nature and nurture no doubt worked hand in hand. He tells us that he was quite deflated in 1972 when he found that his election opponent would be McGovern, whom he felt sure that he could beat easily. He had looked forward to a really hard contest and was quite disappointed at missing one. A combative Quaker. It sounds like a contradiction in terms – that, however, was Richard Nixon.

There was still another side to his Quaker inheritance. His father had been more or less a worldly failure. He felt that the best service he could render to his father or to his father's memory was to succeed where his father had failed. And certainly his progress to fame brought much satisfaction to his father while he was alive. We rightly respect Lord Mountbatten's life-long determination to compensate for his father's forced resignation as First Sea Lord in 1914 owing to his German ancestry. We must respect Richard Nixon likewise.

From his mother he learned a lesson which in certain ways fanned the flame of his ambition, in spite of her warnings to him already quoted. When she was dying and could hardly speak, he managed to blurt out, 'Mother, don't give up.' He himself was going through one of his difficult periods. Her voice became strong as she called to him, 'Richard, don't *you* give up; don't let anyone tell you you are through!' This 'guts' standard (if one can use that expression), this idea of not quitting, exercized a dominant influence over his whole nature. If it was pride, it was the kind of pride which leads men to win the highest decorations for valour.

Elliot Richardson, the Attorney-General who, in 1973, did him, unwittingly, untold damage by appointing Archibald Cox as Special Prosecutor with unlimited terms of reference, used the convenient jargon of sophisticated liberals in a passage quoted earlier. He refers to Nixon's 'insecurity' as something obvious to all persons of intelligence. The trouble about that label is that it is used so widely and indiscriminately. It has been applied to almost all the political leaders of modern times who were possessed of driving ambition, from Hitler to Churchill to Harold Wilson.

Nixon was well aware when he spoke to David Frost that the word 'paranoia' was frequently attached to him. But it is not denied today that he was bitterly and unendingly attacked. Richardson bears witness to it in the passage quoted. Most dispassionate persons would concede that he was *unfairly* attacked by the media for many years. A gifted young woman on the *New York Times* said to me recently when I told her that I had just written a book about Nixon: 'You must realize that I was brought up [this would have been before Watergate] to believe that Richard Nixon was the devil incarnate.' He had at least something substantial to be paranoid about.

Take this passage, for example, from David Halberstam (*The Powers That Be*, page 598), whose fascinating book on the influence of the American media is unremittingly harsh towards Nixon: 'By 1972 it appeared that the Nixon campaign against the press had been more than partially successful; the great newspapers and broadcasting corporations seemed on the defensive, the Administration's technical skills in using television seemed greater and greater (there were those who suspected that the Nixon administration used bombing as a weapon in the continuation of the war rather than ground troops because among other things, television did not cover bombing raids).'

It could be argued at least as plausibly that, in the long escalating hostility between Nixon and leading elements in the media, it was the latter who were basically the aggressors. It is noticeable moreover that John Kennedy's superb handling of television is treated by Halberstam as altogether delightful; Nixon's efforts in that direction, aided by Haldeman, as positively sinister.

Let us, however, concede that there was a flaw here – psychological if not moral. Did it help to explain the dark side which some of those who admired him, and still admire him, refer to? Safire, Price, Colson, Haldeman – they all agree that the dark side was not the real Nixon but that it represented a lurking menace. Theodore White justly comments that the American presidential system had been coming under growing pressure for at least twenty years. The huge responsibilities at home and abroad were becoming huger still while the party system grew steadily weaker. He sees them as bearing down on a personality in Richard Nixon whose flaws of character would, inevitably, let him down in the crisis, but it seems to me too facile to assume that he was more flawed for political purposes than some of his immediate predecessors. British Prime Ministers are not subjected to quite so intense a personal scrutiny but most British premierships, in recent years, beginning with those of Macdonald, Baldwin and Chamberlain, are looked back on today without admiration though, it must be said, without charges of perfidy.

When he delivered his final address before resignation, Nixon said some moving words about the destructive power of hatred. He was no doubt speaking there of what he had himself experienced, and returning to the simplicities of his Quaker upbringing. Chuck Colson, in his new book *Life Sentence*, tells the story of his having criticized Henry Kissinger on television after his release from prison. He was rung up by Nixon unexpectedly. 'I caught some excerpts', said the ex-President, 'of your interview on the "Today Show" and, uh, well, Henry called me. . . . You know we only have one President now. One Secretary of State. So we need to support them, you know, Chuck. They are all we have. I mean, you and I know Henry's faults, but as Americans we support our leaders and our country, right?'

This, comments Colson, was Richard Nixon at his best. For all his faults, including those which had toppled his presidency, he deeply loved his country. He adds something which must have some significance from a former aide whose association with Nixon landed him in prison: 'Few historians will credit Nixon with having a warm heart, but I believe otherwise.' Bill Gulley supports it on page after page.

Nixon was adored by his family. Tricia, at the darkest of moments, referred to him in her diary as always thinking of others. Even the chilly reviewer of his book in the *New York Times* made the concession: 'His wife and daughters' extraordinary loyalty to him must reflect to some degree the father's kindliness and thoughtfulness within the family circle.' The letter to Terry Eagleton quoted above is only one example of his capacity for sensitive understanding.

Still, he went down calamitously. Bad luck came in somewhere, but some further explanation is necessary. It is tempting to discover some fatal weakness in his character which was bound to lead to his political destruction. I would rather argue that the circumstances in which he was actually placed as President bore down heavily on what was at once his strongest and his weakest point – his burning desire to leave a glorious mark on history. No Republican president at that moment would have achieved the restructuring of American government which he dreamed of. He went on regardless of the inevitable obstacles and hostilities. And Vietnam did the rest. On the deeper issues he was thin-skinned. He was sufficiently a man of conscience to savour the full pain of tragedy when it came to him and through his actions to those he loved.

One's mind goes back to Macaulay's famous essay on Warren Hastings, the most distinguished Englishman to be impeached. At the end he leaves Hastings 'in peace after so many wars, in honour after so much obloquy'. It may be some years before the same can be said of Richard Nixon. It may not happen in his lifetime. Meanwhile he survives, his longing to be great possibly quenched but not, I would think, his thirst for nobility. I would hope and believe that he would end his life as a man who would have been approved of by his father and, with suitable warnings, his mother.

He comes before us now with the gravest of warnings. The thesis of his latest book *The Real War* (1980) can be stated baldly in the following propositions:

1) Soviet ambitions will continue to be remorselessly aggressive; their unremitting purpose the absorption of the whole world.
2) They confront the free world in general and in particular the United States, its main bulwark, with a challenge of global proportions and ever greater urgency.
3) An adequate counter to Soviet imperialism cannot be provided by the United States alone, but without strong United States leadership, above all presidential leadership, it cannot be provided at all.
4) Since the Kennedy–Khrushchev confrontation of 1962, the military position of the USA relative to the Soviet Union has steadily worsened – most notably since Nixon resigned the presidency in 1974.
5) If present trends continue, the Soviet Union will be in a position by 1985 to dictate surrender terms to the USA.
6) It is still possible for the West to avert catastrophe, but only if there is a radical change of attitude and if a much greater proportion of resources is devoted to defence.

President Nixon is as firm as ever in his belief in detente which is complementary to parity in defence. Without détente there can be little progress towards permanent peace; without parity in defence, there can be no survival for the West. We shall neglect his warning at our extreme peril.

Select Bibliography

Agnew, Spiro, *Go Quietly ... Or Else*. New York: Wm Morrow, 1980

Colby, William, *Honourable Men: My Life in the C.I.A.* London: Hutchinson, 1978

Colson, Charles W., *Born Again*. London: Hodder & Stoughton, 1976

—— *Life Sentence*. Lincoln, Virginia: Chosen Books, 1979

Dean, John, *Blind Ambition*. New York: Simon & Schuster, 1976

Ford, Gerald, *A Time to Heal*. New York: Harper & Row & Readers' Digest Association Inc., 1979

Frost, David, *I Gave Them a Sword: Behind the Scenes of the Nixon Interviews*. London: Macmillan London Limited, 1978

Goldwater, Barry, *With No Apology*. New York: Wm Morrow, 1979

Gulley, Bill, with Mary Ellen Reese, *Breaking Cover*. New York: Simon & Schuster, 1980

Halberstam, David, *The Powers That Be*. London: Chatto & Windus, 1979

Haldeman, H. R., and DiMona, Joseph, *The Ends of Power*. London: Sidgwick & Jackson, 1978

Hunt, E. Howard, *Undercover – Memoirs of an American Secret Agent*. London: W. H. Allen, 1975

Jaworski, Leon, *The Right and the Power – The Prosecution of Watergate*. New York: Pocket Books, 1977

Kissinger, Henry, *The White House Years*. London: Weiden-feld & Nicolson and Michael Joseph, 1979

Kurland, P.B., *Watergate and the Constitution*. Chicago: University of Chicago Press, 1977

Lasky, Victor, *It Didn't Start with Watergate*. New York: The Dial Press, 1977

Liddy, G. Gordon, *Will*. New York: St Martin's Press, 1980

Moynihan, Daniel Patrick with Suzanne Weaver, *A Dangerous Place*. London: Secker & Warburg, 1979

New York Times, Staff of the, *The End of a Presidency*. New York: Bantam Books, 1974

Nixon, Richard, *The Memoirs of Richard Nixon*. London: Sidgwick & Jackson, 1978

—— *The Real War*. London: Sidgwick & Jackson, 1980

Price, Raymond, *With Nixon*. New York: The Viking Press, 1977

Richardson, Elliot, *The Creative Balance*. London: Hamish Hamilton, 1976

Safire, William L., *Before the Fall*. New York: Doubleday, 1975

Schlesinger, Arthur M., Jr., *Robert Kennedy and His Times*. London: Andre Deutsch, 1978

Shawcross, William, *Sideshow – Kissinger, Nixon and the Destruction of Cambodia*. London: Andre Deutsch, 1979

Thompson, F. D., *At That Point in Time – The Inside Story of the Senate Watergate Committee*. New York: Quadrangle/The New York Times Book Co., 1975.

White, Theodore H. *The Making of the President 1960*. New York: Atheneum, 1961

—— *The Making of the President 1962*. New York: Atheneum, 1963

—— *The Making of the President 1964*. New York: Atheneum, 1965

—— *The Making of the President 1968*. New York: Atheneum, 1969

—— *The Making of the President 1972*. New York: Atheneum, 1973

—— *Breach of Faith*. New York: Atheneum, 1975

Witcover, J., *The Resurrection of Richard Nixon*. New York: G. P. Putnam, 1970

Woodward, Bob, and Bernstein, Carl. *All the President's Men*. New York: Simon & Schuster, 1974

Woodward, Bob, and Bernstein, Carl. *The Final Days*. London: Secker & Warburg, 1976

Impeachment of Richard M. Nixon, President of the United States, Final Report by the House of Representatives Judiciary Committee, August 1974

Index

INDEX

INDEX